THE FIRST
FRANCISCANS
and
THE GOSPEL

THE FIRST
FRANCISCANS
and
THE GOSPEL

•

By Duane V. Lapsanski

FRANCISCAN HERALD PRESS
1434 WEST 51st STREET • CHICAGO, 60609

The First Franciscans and the Gospel   by Duane V. Lapsanski. Copyright © 1976 by Franciscan Herald Press, 1434 West 51st Street, Chicago, Illinois 50509. All rights reserved.

Library of Congress Cataloging in Publication Data:

Lapsanski, Duane V
    The first Franciscans and the Gospel.

    Translation of Das Leben nach dem Evangelium am Anfang des Minderbruderordens.
    Bibliography: p.
    Includes index.
    1. Franciscans—Spiritual life. I. Title
BX3603.L3513   255'.3   75-8685
ISBN 0-8199-0568-2

Nihil Obstat:
    Mark Hegener O.F.M.
    Censor Deputatus

Imprimatur:
    Msgr. Richard A. Rosemeyer, J.C.D.
    Vicar General, Archdiocese of Chicago

January 14, 1976

MADE IN THE UNITED STATES OF AMERICA

To my parents
Margaret and Andrew

Table of Contents

List of Abbreviations

ActaSS	Acta Sanctorum (Antwerp, then Brussels, 1643-1894) 67 vols. [Original edition].
AnalFranc	Analecta Franciscana sive Chronica aliaque varia Documenta ad historiam Fratrum Minorum spectantia, edita a Patribus Collegii s. Bonaventurae (Quaracchi, 1885 ff.).
ArchFrancHist	Archivum Franciscanum Historicum (Quaracchi, 1908 ff.).
BullFr	Bullarium Franciscanum, I, ed. J. H. Sbaralea (Rome, 1759).
CollFranc	Collectanea Franciscana (Rome, 1931 ff.).
EtudFranc	Etudes franciscaines (Paris, 1899).
FranzStud	Franziskanische Studien (Munster, then Werl i. W., 1914 ff.).
FStudies	Franciscan Studies (St. Bonaventure, N.Y., 1940 ff.).
Leg 3 Comp	Legend of the Three Companions, in: Omn, pp. 887-955.
MGSS	*Monumenta Germaniae Historica. Scriptores.* 30 vols. New York-Stuttgart, 1963ff.
Omn	St. Francis of Assisi: Writings and Early Biographies: English Omnibus of the Sources for the Life of St. Francis, ed.

ix

	Marion A. Habig (Chicago: Franciscan Herald Press, 1972).
PL	Patrologia Latina, ed. J. P. Migne (Paris, since 1844).
RGG	*Religion in Geschichte und Gegenwart.* 6 vols. 3rd rev. ed. (Tübingen, 1957-1965).
TestMin	Testimonia Minora saeculi XIII de s. Francisco Assisiensi, ed. L. Lemmens (Quaracchi, 1926).
Four Masters	Expositio quatuor magistrorum super regulam Fratrum Minorum (1241-1242), ed. L. Oliger (Rome, 1950).
WissWeish	Wissenschaft und Weisheit (Dusseldorf, 1934 ff.).

Preface

Recently I published a study dealing with the concept of "evangelical perfection" in the early franciscan sources.[1] In the second part of that work I approached each source with questions of this sort in my mind, "What is the essence of franciscan life according to this source? What are the fundamental values which animated the primitive franciscan community according to this author?" As a result of this dialogue with the texts, I was able to extract from each source its specific view of the franciscan way of life, which I then summarized in individual chapters of my book. In the course of my study I came to realize that each specific view or construct of the franciscan life was composed of a number of important motifs, such as Gospel Life, the Following of Christ, Fraternity, Nature and Mission of the Order, Poverty, etc. As might be expected, many of these motifs kept recurring in source after source.

What became evident to me, however, was that this recurrence did not automatically mean stale repetition. More often than not each author added his own modifications to the theme, so much so that when I examined a particular motif in two or more different sources, I could usually pinpoint a change of viewpoint or stress, an expansion or a narrowing of the theme from source to source. For example, the theme of "Gospel Life" plays an important role in the writings of St. Francis. In the later sources, Francis' under-standing of this theme is at times faithfully preserved; but at other times it is re-interpreted to fit new life-situations, or even lost sight of altogether.[2]

It then occurred to me that if one were to trace the chron-ological evolution which the above mentioned themes under-went from source to source, one might well hope to compose a fascinating mosaic depicting the life and values of the primitive franciscan brotherhood. And that is precisely what I have tried to do in the present book. My aim, as is evi-dent, is not to present a systematic and well-rounded study of each theme, but rather to share with the reader some of the dynamic insights which the early sources contain and to indicate the evolution which many of these themes under-went during the early decades of franciscan history. As such, this book can provide an introduction to the study of key franciscan themes and values. In particular, it can serve as a map showing the reader where to begin and what to look for when he or she cracks open the big, red, ominous-looking *Omnibus of Sources.*[3]

If this book needs further justification, let it be this: the present study is based on the sources which were written during the earliest decades of the franciscan movement. These sources, more than any other writings, put us in touch with the original vision of the Christian life as taught and in-carnated by Francis. Many of the existing books on francis-can ideals and spirituality, on the contrary, were based, in large measure, on sources which were written during the last quarter of the thirteenth, and even during the fourteenth, century and thus reflect the viewpoints and controversies of those decades. Going to these later sources for an under-standing of the franciscan charism is somewhat like basing one's view of Christ and the Christian life not on the canon-ical Gospels and Epistles but on midrash and the apocrypha.

This English version is more than a translation of the original study. I have taken the liberty of rewriting and expanding many of the passages, so as to "round-out" thoughts which were expressed too succinctly in the original. I have also added a number of citations from the Bible, particularly from the Psalms and from the Epistles of St. Paul. This I have done in order to indicate how beautifully the values expressed in the early franciscan sources mesh with and complement the spiritual insights of God's written Word. Finally, I have simplified the notes substantially by eliminating Latin quotes and many references to works in foreign languages. In order to avoid the need of constantly flipping pages to find the notes, I have included many references in the body of the text.

* * * *

If the glimpses which these pages offer into the life and values of the early franciscan community stimulate a handful of modern friars to be as conscious of their lofty mission and to become as open to God and neighbor as were the first Lesser Brothers, this book shall have achieved its purpose. And if the portrait of Francis here presented stimulates one or another modern son or daughter to become the kind of person that Francis was and to fill the needs of the contemporary world with as much understanding, love and concern as he did, the author shall have been richly rewarded!

D. V. L.

The Franciscan Institute
St. Bonaventure, N.Y. 14778
Feast of the Conversion of St. Paul
January 25, 1976

Introduction

Life according to the "perfection of the Gospels" has unfolded within the Church of Jesus Christ with great richness during the long centuries of its existence. In the following pages I will sketch the way in which this Christian life was lived and interpreted within a small segment of Christ's Church, namely the Franciscan Order, and during a brief span of that long history, roughly the decades extending from 1210 through 1260. Because it is to the early franciscan sources that I have recourse so often, I wish first of all to list and to describe these sources briefly, but also to indicate the relative value of each. The most important ones for my study are the following:

1. The Writings of St. Francis of Assisi

These were composed for the most part in the last several years of the saint's life and include the two extant Rules of the Order of Friars Minor, the Testament, as well as admonitions, letters, praises and prayers. For our study these writings have a fundamental importance, for they contain the most authentic summary and description of the life to which God called Francis. They also provide a valuable norm against which later interpretations and views of the franciscan ideal can be measured, judged, and criticized. (*Omn*, 23–167)

2. Encyclical Letter of Brother Elias on the Death of Francis[4]

This is the official letter which Elias of Cortona sent to the "Minister of the Brothers" in France and very likely to all the provinces as well in order to formally announce the death of St. Francis. In this masterpiece of theological reflection, Elias places Francis and his brotherhood squarely within the context of Salvation History: he views the saint and his companions as special instruments which God is using to bring about the salvation of many.

3. St. Francis and His Lady Poverty

This work, which an unknown franciscan composed very likely as early as 1227, can best be characterized as a medieval "Mystery Play." Not only is the *Sacrum Commercium* an important indicator of the spirituality and idealism of the early franciscan community, but it is also an enticing piece of literature, since it so effectively fuses biblical theology with feudal imagery. (*Omn,* 1531–96)

4. The Biographies of St. Francis by Thomas of Celano

Around the time of the canonization of St. Francis, Pope Gregory IX commissioned Friar Thomas of Celano to write an official biography of the new saint. In all likelihood, this first biography was completed toward the end of 1228, or, at the latest, in the early weeks of 1229. Not long after, probably in 1230, Celano composed a *Legenda ad usum chori,* which is basically a short summary of the *Vita I.* Following the General Chapter of Genoa, the newly-elected Minister General, Crescentius of Jesi, commissioned Thomas of Celano to write a new biography of St. Francis. This the author did, in all probability between August 1246 and May 1247, by using unpublished material which the friars had recently submitted to the General. This second life (*Vita II*) is not a biography in the ordinary sense of the word, but rather a supplement to the *Vita I.*

Because the *Vita II* reported too few miracles, the new Minister General, John of Parma (1247-57), commissioned the author to collect and to put into writing the many reports of miracles performed by St. Francis during his lifetime as well as those attributed to his intercession after his death. This work, aptly titled *The Treatise on the Miracles of St. Francis,* Celano completed before the end of 1252.[5] The first chapters of this work are of particular importance for the present study, for they contain a theological meditation on the significance of the Order of Friars Minor and of St. Francis himself within the context of Salvation History.

Unfortunately, the *Legenda major* of St. Bonaventure has overshadowed the writings of Thomas of Celano since the last part of the thirteenth century. In the last part of the nineteenth century, however, modern critical research has "rediscovered" these legends, so that today they, together with the writings of Francis himself, are considered to be the "foundation stone for the life of the great Saint of Assisi and for the early history of the franciscan movement."[6]

In connection with the early franciscan sources the word "legend" appears frequently. This term may give the modern reader some trouble, since to us the word "legend" ordinarily refers to stories or events which are not authenticated by history. The meaning this term had in the Middle Ages, however, was far different. At that time the word was used to indicate the life and deeds of the martyr or confessor which *were to be read* (*L. Legenda*) on the saint's feast. The term in no way indicated that the account was not historical. Thus, the "legends" of St. Francis written by Thomas of Celano, by St. Bonaventure, by the Three Companions, etc., are not tales or fables about the saint, but an account of his life and deeds. The present study uses the word "legend" in this medieval sense.

5. Julian of Speyer

Julian, a friar of accomplished literary, poetic and musical ability, composed an office for the feast of St. Francis[7] (1231-32), in which he extolled the works of the saint in epic fashion. Some years later, certainly before 1235, Julian wrote a life of St. Francis.[8] Although this legend is primarily a summary of Celano's *Vita I,* it is an important work in its own right, for Julian greatly expanded Celano's tendency of using the static and abstract term "evangelical perfection" in order to interpret the life of the Friars Minor. He thereby helped to push Francis' understnading of the concrete and dynamic "evangelical life" out of the friars' immediate consciousness.[9]

6. The Legend of the Three Companions

This is not a biography in the usual sense of the word but rather the vivid memories which three of St. Francis' companions, namely, Leo, Angelo, and Rufino, wrote down and sent to the Minister General at the request of the General Chapter of 1244. Not only does the legend contain an excellent description of the way in which St. Francis and his earliest companions lived, but it is also an important and unprejudiced source for the early history of the Order.[10] (*Omn,* 853-955)

7. Early Liturgical Texts

In the first decades following the death of St. Francis there arose a series of liturgical texts which shed some light on the events and significance of the saint's vocation. For the sake of convenience these texts can be classifed into three categories, namely, breviary lessons,[11] sequences,[12] and Masses.[13] Though these texts contain no new historical data, they are important for our study, for they reveal which events and aspects of St. Francis the first friars found significant enought to "celebrate" in their official liturgy.

8. Writings by and about St. Clare[14]

Under this heading are included two categories of writings and documents. The first consists of those writings which St. Clare herself authored, namely, The Rule and Testament of St. Clare, four letters and a blessing to Agnes of Prague and a letter to Ermentrude of Brugge. The second category contains writings to or about St. Clare, namely, the Life of St. Clare, written by Thomas of Celano (1255); the Privilege of Seraphic Poverty, issued by Pope Innocent III in 1215 and repeated by Pope Gregory IX in 1228; the Bull of Canonization of St. Clare (1225); the letter of Agnes of Prague to St. Clare (ca. 1229); Cardinal Hugolin's letter to Clare (1220); a Letter by Pope Gregory IX to the Poor Clares (1228); and the Encyclical Letter on the death of St. Clare.

These writings are important, for they reveal the spirituality, the life-style and the ideals of the saint who rightly called herself "a handmaid of our Lord Jesus Christ, a plant of our most holy Father Saint Francis."[15]

9. The Commentary on the Rule by the Four Masters[16]

In response to a request made by the General Chapter of Definitors (1241) that each province compile disputed questions and points of doubt concerning the observance of the Rule, four masters of theology at Paris set down in writing their views and solutions to the controversial issues then under debate by the friars. The four masters, Alexander of Hales, John de la Rochelle, Robert of Bastia and Odo Rigaldus, did not intend to describe the ideals of the friars, nor even to interpret the entire Rule. Their primary concern was rather to present canonically acceptable solutions to the nagging problems connected with the external observance of the Rule in the daily life of the friars. Though legalistically oriented, the four masters uncovered and respected the true "intention" of the Rule of St. Francis.

10. The Commentary on the Rule by Hugh of Digne[17]

Between 1245 and the year of his death (ca. 1255) Hugh of Digne, a learned and courageous French friar, wrote an extended exposition of the Rule of the Friars Minor in which he sought to explain and defend the Rule against those who found it too strict and too difficult to observe. In the pages of this well thought-out exposition, Hugh reveals not only his firm convictions and deep spirituality, but above all a vibrant love for the Gospel, which he considered to be the very core of the friars' way of life. What Hugh did in this commentary was to rekindle in the minds of his contemporaries St. Francis' vision of the "Life according to the Gospel."

11. The Chronicle of Jordan of Giano[18]

This early franciscan classic contains the oft-repeated, jolly and vivid recollections of an old man who spent more than forty-five years in the Order. This Chronicle, written down around 1262, describes a number of significant events connected with the early history of the Order of Friars Minor and particularly the hardships and adventures experienced by the brothers who came to establish the Order in Germany.

Jordan's recollections are important because they offer us a direct glimpse into the life-style and the attitudes of the brothers, as well as their enthusiasm in spreading the Gospel.

12. The Chronicle of Thomas of Eccleston[19]

In this work Brother Thomas offers the reader a veritable mine of accurate information concerning the arrival and the first thirty years of the Friars Minor in England. Thomas collected his material over a period of some twenty-six years and completed its writing in 1258 or shortly thereafter. He was particularly interested in recording the holy sayings and the noble deeds of the pioneer friars in England in order to inspire his contemporaries to follow their example. His interpretation of the life of the Friars Minor and his description of the English Province, however, have such a strongly "monastic" tone, that the "Life according to the Gospel" which Francis lived and taught is barely noticeable.

13. The Chronicle of Salimbene de Adam[20]

This chronicle, justly called the "most remarkable autobiography of the Middle Ages,"[21] not only describes the mores of medieval society, but also analyzes the dynamics of its inner life. Within a broad sociological framework, the author sketches the development of the Order of Friars Minor, its heroism, and its pettiness. Salimbene himself shows very little understanding of, and even less sympathy for, Francis' view of the "Life according to the Gospel." Himself a refined gentleman of noble stock, Salimbene wished the Friars Minor to evolve quickly into a well-organized and respected Order capable of carrying out a wide variety of ecclesiastical and even political missions on behalf of the Church.

14. Papal Documents

The documents here in question, all contained in the first volume of the *Bullarium Franciscanum*,[22] span the pontificates of three popes, namely Honorius III (1216–27), Gregory IX (1227–41), and Innocent IV (1243–.54). For the most part these documents deal with a wide range of topics, as for example, exemptions, indulgences, privileges, canonizations, etc., and tend to interpret the life of the Friars Minor in terms of "monastic" categories. At the same time, the documents do offer some keen insights into the friars' Gospel life, as well as into the personality and mission of St. Francis.

15. Sources outside the Order[23]

Under this heading are included a wide variety of 13th century chronicles, legends of saints, sermons and letters which were written by persons not belonging to the Order of Friars Minor but which nevertheless contain references to Francis and his companions. Since some of these references are actual eye-witness accounts, they offer a direct, unreflected glimpse into the earliest years of the Order, that is, how the friars appeared to the people who came in contact with them. More importantly, because these sources have no "family" interests to protect, they can be presumed to be unbiased and by-and-large objective witnesses. As such they can serve as a valuable "control" on the sources which originated within the Order itself. (Omn, 1597–11617).

* * * *

The year 1257 serves as a convenient *terminus ad quem* for this study, since that is when St. Bonaventure was elected Minister General of the Order. With this great thinker and writer there began a new generation of sources which created a new synthesis of the franciscan ideal and therefore merit a separate and thorough study. The Chronicles of Jordan of Giano, Thomas of Eccleston, and Salimbene de Adam, though written after 1257, are nonetheless included in this study because they are unbiased and contain much information about and valuable insights into the earliest decades of the Order.

It is important to note that the franciscan movement, as indeed all historical movements, can be understood rightly and adequately only if it is viewed within its historical context. In the case of the franciscan movement the historical context includes the many efforts to renew the Church exerted by numerous zealous Christians over a span of some hundred and fifty years prior to the time of St. Francis. For the sake of clarity this century and a half can be broken up into three phases or stages of reform. The first stage took place during the second half of the eleventh century and concerned itself with the renewal of already existing ecclesiastical institutions. It was during this time that the Gregorian Reform was launched; writers such as Peter Damian, Rupert of Deutz and Hugh of St. Victor attempted to reform the lifes of monks and Canons Regular.

The second stage of reform took place during the opening decades of the twelfth century. This age was characterized by the rise of *new* ecclesiastical communities, such as the Order of Grandmont, founded by Stephan of Thiers-Muret, and especially a group of itinerant preachers in France. These men, for example, Robert of Arbrissel, Bernard of Thiron, Vitalis of Savigny, Gerald of Salles, and Norbert of Gennep, decided to observe strict poverty and to go about the countryside preaching penance. They did this in an effort to observe the demands of the Gospel in a very literal fashion. The third stage of reform covers the final third of the twelfth and the opening decade of the thirteenth centuries. During this time zealous *lay* Christians, both men and women, became enthusiastic about the simple life of the Gospels and formed communities in which they tried to incarnate their ideals. The Waldenses, the Humiliati, the Poor Catholics, and the Community of Bernard Primus are good examples of this phase of renewal.

Francis and Dominic, it is clear by now, did not come on the scene like a bolt out of the blue. Rather, they may best be considered as the summation and indeed the highpoint of this long effort of renewal extending from roughly 1050 till 1210. In order to better understand the franciscan community and its values, I shall make references in the course of this study to these three phases of renewal, by pointing out similarities or differences, as the case may be, between the early franciscans and their predecessors.[24]

Notes

Preface and Introduction

1. Duane V. Lapsanski, *Perfectio evangelica. Eine Begriffsgeschichtliche Untersuchung im fruhfranziskanischen Schrifttum* (Paderborn: F. Schoningh, 1974). I am planning to publish an English edition of this study.

2. Ibid., pp. 239-70.

3. Marion A. Habig, ed., *St. Francis of Assisi: Writings and Early Biographies. English Omnibus of the Sources for the Life of St. Francis* (Chicago: Franciscan Herald Press, 1972). This book is hereafter referred to as Omn, followed by the page number. Wherever advisable I shall make references to this book within the text itself, in order not to multiply unduly the number ot notes.

4. The most accurate English translation of Elias' encyclical letter is found in Auspicius van Corstanje, *The Convenant with God's Poor*, trans. G. Reidy, rev. S. A. Yonick (Chicago: Franciscan Herald Press, 1966,), pp. 125-128.

5. The English translation of the *Vita I* is found in Omn, 227-355; that of the *Vita II* in Omn, 359-543. Only selections of the *Treatise on the Miracles of the Blessed Francis* are found in Omn, 547-544; the complete Latin text is found in AnalFranc X, 269-330. Henceforth these writings of Thomas of Celano will generally be referred to as 1 Celano, 2 Celano, and 3 Celano respectively, followed by the paragraph number. The text of the *Legenda ad usum chori* is to be found in AnalFranc X, 118-26.

6. Englebert Grau, *Thomas von Celano: Leban und Wunder des hl. Franziskus von Assisi* (Werl, Westf.: Dietrich-Coelde-Verlag, 1964), p. 27.

7. The *Officium rhythmicum s. Francisci* is found in AnalFranc X, 372-88.

8. The *Vita s. Francisci* is found in AnalFranc X, 334-71.

9. Lapsanski, pp. 253-56.

10. The heated controversy concerning the authorship and date of

composition of this source, as well as its relationship to other franciscan sources, has not yet been laid to rest. I accept the viewpoint of Clasen that this legend precedes 2 Celano. See Sophronius Clasen and Engelbert Grau, *Die Dreigefahrtenlegende des hl. Franziskus. Die Bruder Leo, Rufin und Angelus erzahlen vom Anfang seines Ordens* (Werl, Westf.: Dietrich-Coelde-Verlag, 1972), pp. 94-164. This legend will be referred to as Leg 3 Comp.

11. AnalFranc X, 531-54.

12. AnalFranc X, 397-404.

13. AnalFranc X, 389-96.

14. Ignatius Brady, ed. and trans., *The Legend and Writings of St. Clare of Assisi: Introduction: Translation: Studies* (St. Bonaventure, N. Y.: Franciscan Institute, 1953).

15. *The Blessing of St. Clare* (Brady, p. 100).

16. L. Oliger, ed., *Expositio quatuor magistrorum super regulam Fratrum Minorum (1241-1242)* (Rome, 1950). Henceforth this source sill be cited as Four Masters.

17. Hugh of Digne, *Expositio super regulam Fratrum Minorum,* preserved in the Archives of the O.F.M. Conv., cod. 258, fol. 1r-66r. I wish to express my sincere thanks to David Flood for his kind permission to use his transcription of the manuscript for my study. Hugh's commentary can also be found in the following early prints: Monumenta Ordinis Minorum (Salamanca, 1505), III, fol. 45r-75v; Firmamentum Trium Ordinum s. Francisci, (Paris, 1512), IV, fol. 34v-54v.

18. The English translation of this chronicle is found in Placid Hermann, trans., *XIIIth Century Chronicles: Jordan of Giano, Thomas of Eccleston, Salimbene degli Adami* (Chicago: Franciscan Herald Press, 1961), pp. 17-72.

19. Hermann, pp. 91-191.

20. Hermann, pp. 217-290, contains only selections of Salimbene's Chronicle. The complete Latin text is found in G. Scalia, ed., *Cronica* (Bari, 1966).

21. G. G. Coulton, *From St. Francis to Dante* (London, 1906), p. 1.

22. J. H. Sbaralea, ed., Bullarium Franciscanum, I (Rome, 1759). This volume will henceforth be cited as BullFr.

23. The best collection of these sources is that by L. Lemmens, ed., *Testimonia Minora saeculi XIII de s. Francisco Assisiensi.* This volume is henceforth cited as TestMin.

24. For information concerning each of these movements see Lapsanski, pp. 1-43.

1.

THE EXPERIENCE OF GOD
AS THE FOUNDATION
OF THE FRIARS' GOSPEL LIFE

The Experience of God

A careful reading of the early franciscan sources reveals that the dynamism which powered the life of St. Francis and that of his followers was provided by the all-good, almighty, eternal and loving God. This is not merely to say that the brothers and sisters had abstract knowledge *about* God, that he exists, is the source of life and all created reality, etc. What the sources stress, and very dramatically so, is that the primitive community enjoyed a very personal and vivid *experience* of God as loving Father.

1. "The Lord Inspired Me, Brother Francis"

Though many beautiful and meaningful words have been spoken and continue to be spoken about Francis of Assisi, the fundamental truth about this simple and fascinating man is that at the very core of his being and at the very center of his life, he was filled with God. Certainly one of the most exciting aspects of St. Francis, as so many of his writings testify, is that he actually met and experienced God in his life and surrendered himself to Him completely. His Testament (Omn, 67–68) rings out with the firm conviction that it was the *Lord* himself who revealed to him the kind of life he was to live. It was the *Lord,* Francis repeats over and over again in this autobiography, who inspired him to do penance, that is, to undergo the process of *metanoia:* of turning away from one's previous attitudes of trusting in self and turning now to God with love and confidence.[1] It was the *Lord* who led him among lepers, who gave him faith in the Church and in priests; it was the *Lord* who gave him brothers, who inspired him to write the rule, and who revealed to him the greeting of peace.

It was upon this firm conviction that the Lord was leading him and acting very intimately in his life that Francis' entire religious vocation was grounded. At the same time Francis was fully convinced that God's action and inspiration were not the result of any merit on his part, but were wholly God's free gift to him. The fifth Amonition expresses Francis' view that life is a gift very well: "Try to realize the dignity God has conferred on you. He created and formed your body in the image of his beloved Son, and your soul in his own likeness" (Omn, 80). In his *Vita II* Thomas of Celano reports that Francis actually called God a gift-giver! With these words Francis encouraged some hungry knights to put away their pride and to place their trust in God when they go begging for alms: "Do not be ashamed, for all things have been given to us as an alms after sin, and that *great Almsgiver* bestows his gifts with loving kindness to the worthy and the unworthy" (2 Celano, 77; Omn, 427).

Conscious of God's presence in his life, Francis desired nothing else than to follow ever more closely the will of God and to ever thank and praise him for his goodness and greatness. So often in the course of his writings Francis' heart literally bursts forth in spontaneous prayer and praise to the Lord. I refer to his heart, for it is not merely Francis' mind or tongue that does the praising, but his whole person. His entire being gets caught up in the act: "With all our hearts and all our souls, all our minds and all our strength, all our power and all our understanding, with every faculty and every effort, with every affection and all our emotions, with every wish and desire, we should love our Lord and God who has given and gives us everything, body and soul, and all our life. . ." (Rule 1221, ch. 23; Omn, 51-52). These are the words of a man who is deeply in love with the Lord.

The early biographies of Francis maintain this same perspective, for they very definitely underscore the saint's intimate experience of God. With conscious emphasis Thomas of Celano interprets Francis' conversion as the dramatic work of God who came into the young man's life and turned him completely inside out. The young Francis "walked about the streets of Babylon," writes Celano solemnly, "until the Lord looked down from heaven and for his name's sake removed his wrath far off and for his praise bridled Francis lest he should perish. The *hand of the Lord* therefore *came upon him* and a change was wrought by the right hand of the Most High. . . ." A long illness came upon Francis and helped deepen this initial conversion of heart, so that "he began to think of things other than he was used to thinking upon."

During the entire process the Lord was with Francis helping him to overcome his old self. At times Francis "tried to flee the hand of God." But slowly he came to be "filled with a new and singular spirit," which he received from the Lord. This new spirit set him "afire with a divine fire and he was not able to hide outwardly the ardor of his mind." By disposition he had always been a jovial, kind and very open person. But now, through the grace of God, he became literally "filled with a certain exquisite joy of which till then he had had no experience" (1 Celano, 2-10; Omn, 230-38). Francis traveled very far in his spiritual journey—and the Lord guided him every step of the way.

In similar fashion the *Legend of the Three Companions* stresses that the Lord in his loving kindness often "touched" and "visited" the young Francis. One such visitation took place when Francis, elected the king of the party, was following his companions along the streets of Assisi. Francis himself was not singing; he was rather "listening very attentively." He was very attuned to his own heart and to the sacrament of the moment. "All of a sudden," the legend cries out with wonder, *"the Lord touched his heart,* filling it with such *surpassing sweetness* that he could neither speak nor move. He could only feel and hear this *overwhelming sweetness* which detached him so completely from all other physical sensations that, as he later said, had he been cut to pieces on the spot he could not have moved" (n. 7; Omn, 896). Having tasted such sweetness, his heart henceforth could find rest and contentment only in the Lord.

As a result of God's action, both sources continue, Francis became transformed interiorly; he began to turn away more and more from his former way of life and to seek the will of God for him. Mightily did he strive "to bend his own will to the will of God" and to pray unceasingly and with great fervor "that the eternal and true God would direct his way and teach him to do his will" (1 Celano, 6; Omn, 234). The young man became so filled with God and so strengthened by the Spirit that what Jesus explained to Nicodemus (Jn 3:1-21) actually took place within Francis. He was "re-born" in the Lord. Even Francis' early "sinfulness, " adds Julian of Speyer as he reflects on God's action in the saint's life, provided an opportunity for God to reveal the depths of his mercy.[2]

This conversion, of course, was no once-and-for-all affair, but was rather an ongoing process, lasting an entire lifetime. With the zeal of a novice and the inspiration of a lover, he often spoke these striking words at the end of his life to his companions: "My brothers, we must *begin* to serve our Lord and God. Until now we have done very little" (Omn, 737). Holy as he was, Francis realized he still had "many miles to go" in his growth in the Lord. And he had the humility and courage to keep on beginning.

2. Sons of the Heavenly Father

The God who acted as tangibly in the life of Francis also directed the lives of his followers. His brothers and sisters, Francis testifies, have entered upon their new way of life at the inspiration of the Lord (Form of Life; Omn, 76). Henceforth they were to concern themselves only about the Lord and to center their lives ever more deeply on his will for them. "We have left the world now," Francis proclaims with finality, "and all we have to do is to be careful to obey God's will and please him" (Rule of 1221, ch. 22; Omn, 47). These dramatic words of Francis do not wish to deny the obvious fact that the friars did many other things as well, such as working, eating, preaching, going about the countryside, etc. These words do, however, put the friars' life into perspective, namely, that their relationship to God was the first and ultimate value in their lives.

This vibrant consciousness that God was to be the center of the friars' lives is also very evident in the Rule of 1223. Indeed, the very first chapter of that Rule opens with the firm declaration that the life of the friars consists in observing "the Holy Gospel of our Lord Jesus Christ." Other chapters of the Rule point out that candidates to this new way of life may dispose of their goods "as God inspires them"; the mending of clothes and fasting is to be done "with God's blessing." The ability to work is viewed by Francis as a "grace," a gift, given to the friars by the Lord. Their religious life consists in "serving God"; they live in poverty and humility "because God made himself poor for us in this world." The brothers have "promised God" to observe the Rule and have renounced their wills "for God's sake"; superiors are to impose penances on sinful friars "as seems best to them before God." And above all else they should desire to have "the spirit of God at work within them" and to pray to God with a heart "free from self-interest" (Omn, 57-64). This way of life which the friars adopted freely is nothing else than their joyful response to the Lord who is so close to them that he offers himself to them as to sons (Letter to a Chapter; Omn, 104). And because they realize they are sons of the

Father, the friars can face all the situations of life not with fear but with confidence and above all with love.

The words of St. Clare of Assisi ring out with a very similar conviction. She, too, was very conscious of the gift-character of life and so encouraged her sisters to "consider the immense benefits which God has conferred" on them. These benefits of the Lord, the first of which is the sisters' religious vocation, are daily renewed, for the generous Lord is actively present in their lives. "Among the many graces *which we have received and continue daily to receive* from the liberality of the Father of mercies (2 Cor 1:3), and for which we must give deepest thanks to our glorious God, our vocation holds first place." It was the Lord, the "most high celestial Father," writes Clare, who "deigned to enlighten my heart by his mercy and grace to do penance."

Clare was also very conscious that the sisters' vocation and life itself has come to them "not by our own merits but only through the *mercy* and *bounteous grace of the Father* of mercies. . . ." Thus she encourages her sisters, in response to God's kindness to them, "to bless the Lord and praise him and to be strenghtened in him more and more to do good."[3] This attitude of openness and thankfulness, joined to contemplation, will help bring about a transformation within them "in the image of the Godhead," as Clare points out to Bl. Agnes. And this will result in actually feeling "what his friends feel in tasting the hidden sweetness which God himself has kept from the beginning for those who love him."[4] What particularly strikes one about these last words is their experiential character. Clare speaks of "feeling" and "tasting" the "sweetness" of the Lord. She could write in this way because she actually did taste the sweetness of the Lord in her own life!

But this is not all. The Lord is active and present not only in the lives of individual brothers and sisters, but in the community as such, as several sources testify. The entire Order of Friars Minor, maintains Thomas of Celano, is in a special way the work of God, for it was he who inspired zealous men to join Francis in his spiritual adventure. "Be strengthened, dear brothers, and rejoice in the Lord, and do not be sad because you seem so few," Celano has Francis say to his first followers, "and do not let either my simplicity or your own dismay you, for, as it has been shown me in truth by the Lord, *God will make us grow into a very great multitude* and will make us increase to the ends of the world" (1 Celano, 27; Omn, 250).

To this, Celano's *Treatise on the Miracles* adds that God's working with Francis was paradoxical, as it was with the patriarch Abraham. The Lord made the Order into a great "nation" by transforming its hopeless poverty into a principle of fecundity, just as he produced new life out of Abraham's ancient body. As a result of God's activity, dedicated men, true "living stones," have hastened from all over the world to join the Order, thereby building it up into a "wondrous temple" of the Lord.[5]

Jordan of Giano, reviewing in his mind the Order's marvelous growth and its great potential for bringing spiritual help to mankind, declares that the Friars Minor are the beneficiaries of God's goodness and wisdom. When he considers the "littleness" and simplicity of the first friars, he pauses to "praise in my heart the goodness of Almighty God," who, in the words of the Apostle Paul, has once again chosen "the foolish things of this world" to put to shame the wise, and "the weak things" to put to shame the strong (1 Cor 1:27). In fact, Jordan's declared purpose in setting down the history of the Order in his chronicle is to remind the friars whence comes their strength, so that they "may glory *in God,* who in his wisdom founded the Order and through his servant Francis set it up as an example to the world, and *not* glory *in man. . . . "*[6]

A similar conviction, namely that God established the Order, endowed it with a special mission and is guiding it in much the same fashion as he guided his people in both the old and the new testaments, led Brother Elias to honor the Friars minor with the title "new People of God,"[7] while the author of the *Sacrum Commercium* called the friars the "elect" and the "sheepfold" of the Lord. [8]

The brothers' consciousness of the Lord's presence in their lives and their confidence in his protection is a realization of the Psalmist's deep faith in the Lord. The friars, too, can well address their Lord in these moving words:

> . . . you hold me by the hand.
> You guide me with your advice,
>   and at the end you will receive me with honor.
> What else do I have in heaven but you?
>   Since I have you, what else do I want on earth?
> My mind and my body may grow weak,
>   but God is my strength;
>   he is all I ever want!
>
> Surely those who abandon you will die,
>   and you will destroy those who are
>   unfaithful to you.
> But as for me, how wonderful to be near God!
>   In the Lord God I find protection,
> to proclaim all that he has done. (Ps 73:23–28)

* * * *

That God is the author of every grace and of religious life is a theme which is evident not only in the franciscan sources, but is noticeable also in the documents pertaining to the pre-franciscan apostolic movements. Of Stephen of Thiers-Muret (d. 1124), the founder of the Order of Grandmont, it was said that God worked through him and manifested him to the peoples of the world.[9] Robert of Arbrissel (ca. 1060–1117), a secular priest who became an itinerant preacher, felt himself sent by the Spirit of God to preach the Gospel to the poor (Lk 4:18). The grace of God was very evidently present in his life and work, declared his biographer.[10] Bernard of Thiron (d.1117), the friend and companion of Robert and later founder of the Order of Thiron, desired no earthly goods whatever, but sought God alone.[11]

After Gerald of Salles (d.1120) left the monastery to become an itinerant preacher, he underwent a conversion which is reminiscent of St. Francis. His biographer reports that "from then on his clothes and food were changed, from then on he began to be even more earnestly and sincerely open to God and self."[12] Speaking of his own vocation, Norbert of Gennep (ca. 1082–1134), the later founder of the Praemonstratensians, declared that he became a preacher of peace not by his own merits, but by the "free grace of God."[13] In somewhat a similar fashion, Peter Waldo, the founder of the Waldenses, felt a strong and direct call from God to give up his possessions, preach the Gospel and to lead an apostolic way of life.[14]

As meaningful as the above statements are, they pale into insignificance when compared to the great stress which the franciscan sources lay on Francis' vivid experience of God, as well as the Lord's intimate relationship to the Friars Minor. Already here, one might conclude, is contained a significant difference in the way St. Francis and his followers viewed their religious vocation as compared to the self-image of these earlier movements.

In the case of Francis and his followers, as the sources clearly point out, the experience of God is at the center of their lives. Whatever else of significance one is led to say about the primitive franciscan community, it must directly or indirectly be based on and flow from this central experience of God. This will become more evident in the following chapters. Francis and his brothers "lived the Gospel," followed in the "footsteps of Christ," built a fraternity and lived in poverty because the Lord in his loving kindness stretched out his hand and "touched" their lives.

Notes

1. For an excellent and extended study of this important theme, see Chrysostomus Dukker, *The Changing Heart: The Penance-Concept of St. Francis of Assisi*, trans. Bruce Malina (Chicago: Franciscan Herald Press, 1959).

2. *Vita s. Francisci*, prologue (AnalFranc X, 335).

3. *Testament of St. Clare* (Brady, pp. 82-88).

4. *Third Letter to Anges of Prague*, 3 (Brady, p. 94).

5. 3 Celano, 1 (AnalFranc X, 271-72).

6. *Chronicle*, prologue (Hermann, pp. 18-19).

7. *Encyclical Letter*, 3 (van Corstanje, p. 126).

8. *Sacrum Commercium*, 57-58 (Omn, 1590).

9. *Vita s. Stephani* (PL 204, 1009 f.).

10. *Vita b. Roberti de Arbrissello* (PL 162, 1055, 1051).

11. *Vita b. Bernardi Tironesis* (PL 127, 1403).

12. *Vita b. Giraldi* (ActaSS, Oct. X, 255).

13. *Vita Norberti Archiepiscopi Magdeburgensis* (Mgss, XII, 676).

14. H. Wolter, "Aufbruch and Tragik der apostolischen Laienbewegung im Mittelalter," in *Geist und Leben*, 30 (1957), 359. See also Berard Marthaler, "The Forerunners of the Franciscans: The Waldenses," in FStudies, 18 (1958), 133–42.

2.
LIFE
ACCORDING TO THE FORM
OF THE HOLY GOSPEL

In his biography of St. Francis, Julian of Speyer states that after the saint surrendered all his material possessions and put aside all cares and anxieties of heart in order to be free for the service of God, he became a "proclaimer of evangelical perfection."[1] Thomas of Celano uses the very same term to indicate that Francis formed his first followers by teaching them "to follow evangelical perfection."[2]

In both instances the term "evangelical perfection" embraces all the values which Francis and his brothers sought to incarnate in their new way of life. This term can therefore be viewed as the all-encompassing category of the franciscan life. Closely related to it are two other very important terms, namely, "to live according to the form of the holy Gospel" and "to follow in the footsteps of Christ." These latter two terms may be considered as specialized and interdependent aspects of the friars' fundamental ideal.

In the following two chapters we shall examine the early sources in order to discover what they have to tell us about the content of these important terms.

1. The Gospel as Life and Rule

Certainly the highpoint of St. Francis' conversion was God's revelation to him that he should live "according to the form of the holy Gospel." It is important to stress, I think, that though this revelation came to Francis in an instantenous flash, it was prepared for by a purifying inner transformation. What happened to Francis was the process of spiritual growth described by Paul to the Romans. "Offer yourselves as a living sacrifice to God," Paul encourages his readers, "dedicated to his service and pleasing to him. This is the true worship that you should offer. Do not conform outwardly to the standards of this world, but let God *transform* you *inwardly* by a complete *change* of mind. *Then*

you will be able to know the will of God—what is good, and
is pleasing to him, and is perfect" (Rom 12:1:1-3). Francis
did offer himself to the Lord as a "living sacrifice," he did
allow himself to be transformed inwardly, a process which
took some years. And then, on the feast of St. Mathias,
1208, Francis did get to know the will of God for him.

This revelation opened up to Francis a radically new *way
of life,*[3] one based on the literal observance of the Gospels.
In his writings the saint described this life which he and his
brothers began to observe at God's inspiration:[4] they sold all
their possessions and gave to the poor; they were content with
a single tunic, cord and trousers; they stayed in churches,
were unlearned and subject to all. Faithfull to the advice
Christ gave to his apostles, the brothers carried nothing on
their journeys, used the salutation of peace, and ate and
drank what was set before them. They did not contend in
words, but were at peace with each other. They shared their
goods with all who asked of them and preached to people
by word and example, admonishing them to turn their
hearts to the Lord. Finally, they fasted, prayed and worked
with their hands.

This simple yet dramatic form of life, centered about the
observance of the three Gospel counsels, was to be lived
within the community of Christ's Church. Francis was certainly conscious of the dangers of hetrodoxy which confronted
his loosely organized brotherhood and to which a number
of contemporary apostolic groups fell prey. He was conscious, too, that only by being faithful to the Church would
the brothers be able to walk the way of Christ.[5] Hence he
wrote this directive in the Rule of 1223: "The ministers, too,
are bound to ask the Pope for one of the cardinals of the
holy Roman Church to be governor, protector, and corrector
of this fraternity so that we may be utterly subject and sub-
missive to the Church. And so, fimly established in the Cath-

olic faith, we may live always according to the poverty, and the humility, and the Gospel of our Lord Jesus Christ, as we have solemnly promised" (ch. 12; Omn, 64).

A number of early biographies of St. Francis remain faithful to the saint's view of the Gospel life. Thomas of Celano, for example, reports an important moment in Francis' life in these dramatic words: ". . .the holy Francis, hearing that the disciples of Christ should not possess gold of silver or money; nor carry along the way scrip, or wallet, or bread, or a staff; that they should not have shoes, or two tunics; but that they should preach the kingdom of God and penance, immediately cried out exultingly: 'This is what I wish, this is what I seek, this is what I long to do with all my heart.' "

What is so striking about these words is that they indicate that Francis is totally present to this moment of inspiration. He listens carefully to what the Lord is saying to him. He becomes filled with joy and plunges into fulfilling this Gospel message. Francis is here acting from the very depths of his being: he finally knows what he wants and he follows his heart. "He immediately put off his shoes from his feet, put aside the staff from his hands, was content with one tunic, and exchanged his leather girdle for a small cord" (1 Celano, 22; Omn, 246-47). He was indeed no "deaf hearer of the Gospel." This literal and enthusiastic observance by Francis of the Lord's "missionary discourse" to his disciples (see Mt 10:5-14; Mk 6:7-12; Lk 9:1-6) was also emphasized, among other sources, by Julian of Speyer,[6] the *Legend of the Three Companions*[7] and Walter of Gisburn.[8]

In a word, Francis and his brothers observed the Gospel by surrendering all their possessions and desires. They did so in order to become *free* for the service of God. Having thus cast away all cares and anxieties of heart, they began to preach peace, penance and the Kingdom of God. It is important to note here that Francis did not stop with the *literal* and *external* observance of the Gospel. He did, of course, go about in shabby clothes, barefoot and without money. But at the same time he went much deeper, for he saw and stressed the need of being innerly free: free of worries, concerns and anxieties of heart, for these choke the Word of God in man. It was this inner freedom that allowed the brothers to be "content" with only one habit and to remain "gladly" in abandoned churches (Testament; Omn, 68). It also allowed them to experience another Gospel value, namely joy in the Lord. "There was great rejoicing among them [the friars]," reports Celano, "when they saw and had nothing that might give them vain or carnal plea- for earthly things, only the divine consolation gave them joy. . . " (1 Celano, 35; Omn, 257).

2. The Gospel of Peace

What is also striking about the friars' Gospel life is that they were eager not only to preach peace but also to bring it about. Already during his captivity at Perugia, Francis proved himself an effective peacemaker by reconciling the irritable knight with the other prisoners.[9] Later, by his presence and preaching he was often able to establish peace where confusion and discord reigned. Thomas of Celano reports: "The Lord gave him a learned tounge, with which he confounded adversaries of truth, refuted the enemies of the cross of Christ, brought back to the right way those who had gone astray, *made peace* with those in discord, and bound together with the bond of charity those who lived in concord. . . . O how often, having put aside his expensive garments and having put on mean ones, and with his feet unshod, he would go about like one of the brothers and ask the terms of *peace.* This he did solicitously *between a man and his neighbor* as often as was necessary and between God and man always" (1 Celano, 99; Omn, 314).

Thomas, the archdeacon of Spalato, who actually heard Francis preach, reports that "throughout his discourse he spoke of the duty of putting an end to hatreds and of arranging a new *treaty of peace.*" Francis was wearing a "ragged habit," his person seemed "insignificant" and his face was not attractive. "But God conferred so much power on his words," the archdeacon continues, "that they brought back *peace* in many a seignorial family torn apart until then by old, cruel, and furious hatreds even to the point of assassinations" (Omn, 1601-2). This peace mission of Francis continued throughout his life. And even on his deathbed he was able to reconcile the civil and religious authorities of Assisi.[10]

This aspect of the Gospel life was not something that began and ended with Francis. He was concerned that all his brothers do the same. "Though Francis wanted his sons *to be at peace with all men* and to conduct themselves as little ones among all", Celano emphasizes, "he taught by his words and showed by his example that they were to be especially humble toward *clerics*" (2 Celano, 146; Omn, 479). The mention of clerics in this text is very significant. At a time when hetrodox apostolic groups were vilifying the clergy, it was especially with these persons that Francis wanted his brothers to live in peace.

Of course peace is not something one can put on or fake. In order to "make peace" one must first be a "man of peace." This is why Francis spoke these striking words to his brothers: "Since you speak *peace,* all the more so must you have it *in your hearts.* Let none be provoked to anger or scandal by you, but rather may they be drawn to *peace* and *good will,* to *benignity* and *concord* through your *gen-*

tleness" (Leg 3 Comp, 58; Omn, 941). He considered these gentle attitudes of heart so important and so in accord with the Gospel life of the friars that he had them included into the Rule of 1223. In their travels about the world, the friars "should not be quarrelsome or take part in disputes with words or criticize others," he says, "but they should be gentle, peaceful, and unassuming, courteous and humble, speaking respectfully to everyone. . . " (ch. 3; Omn, 60).

That peacemaking was the concern not merely of the primitive community but was also practiced by the following generations of friars is a fact attested to by a number of sources. The papal documents, for example, point out that the friars served as legates and messengers of peace to Emperor Frederick, to a sultan, and to the Greek Church to bring about reconciliation with the Church of Rome.[11] Salimbene reports that a Brother Girardus used this simple but effective words to encourage warring factions in Parma to set aside their strife. Another friar was able to reconcile two cities at war, Venice and Bologna. Still others, John of Pian di Carpine in particular, served as peacemakers in the service of the universal Church.[12] All these missions for the sake of peace, it should be stressed, the friars undertook as an integral part of their life "according to the holy Gospel."

3. Gospel Mosaic

To these primary aspects of the friars Gospel life, the sources add also other elements. Thomas of Celano, in both the first and the second biography of St. Francis, points out that the brothers were free to eat and drink what was set before them, a privilege which the Lord himself granted to his preachers (Lk 10:8).[13] Some of the important sources written by non-franciscans, notably Burchard of Usperg[14] and Alberich of Trois-Fontaines,[15] strikingly agree with this view of the friars' evangelical life.

The friars, they report, lived among the people and went about barefoot to preach the Word of God; they worked with their hands, ate and drank what was placed before them, but made no provisions for the morrow. "These poor men of Christ," writes Jacques de Vitry admiringly, "travel about with neither purse, haversack, bread, nor money in their belts; they have neither gold nor silver; they wear no sandals. . . If they are invited to dinner, they eat and drink what is offered them. When they are given an alms in kind, they do not keep it for future use." All this they do not out of a sense of pride of self-sufficiency, Jacques emphasizes, but because they "rely on the generosity and providence of God for their nourishment."[16]

The sources written in later decades, however, tend to dull or even to lose sight of this dynamic, "missionary" aspect of the friars' Gospel life in favor of a more sedentary, ascetical interpretation. *The Legend of the Three Companions*, for example, broadened the concept of evangelical life somewhat by including within its scope such elements as common ownership of goods after the manner of the early Church, generosity to the poor, respect for priests, the recitation of the Divine Office, attendance at Mass and not judging others.[17] St. Clare, on the other hand, noticeably narrowed the concept of evangelical life. For her it was closely bound up with the observance of poverty. Francis "wrote for us a form of life," Clare writes, referring to herself and her sisters, *"especially* that we should *persevere always in holy poverty.* Nor was he content while living to exhort us by many words and examples to the *love* and *observance* of *most holy poverty,* but also gave us many writings that after his death we would in no wise turn aside from it. . . . "[18]

The Four Masters taught that the evangelical life was realized primarily by observing the three counsels. But they also associated such elements as fasting, going barefoot, wearing only poor clothing and making no provisions for the future with the Gospel life of the friars. The evangelical freedom of eating and drinking they did recognize, but, true canonists that they were, they labelled it a concession.[19]

Jordan of Giano associated the Gospel life with the renunciation of possessions, with simplicity of dress and with preaching. These are the elements he stressed in his description of Francis' conversion. "In the year of our Lord 1209, the third year of his conversion," writes Jordan, "upon hearing in the Gospel what Christ said to his disciples when he sent them out to preach, Francis immediately put aside his staff and purse and shoes and changed his garment, putting on the kind the brothers now wear, becoming an *imitator of evangelical poverty* and a *zealous preacher* of the Gospel."[20]

In a beautifull passage of his chronicle reminiscent of the description of the primitive Christian community in the *Acts of the Apostles,* Jordan recounted the evangelical attitudes which reigned in the hearts of the brothers gathered at a General Chapter. "Who can explain," he asks with wonder, "how great was the charity among the brothers at this time and the patience, humility, obedience, and brotherly cheerfulness?"[21] Jordan must have certainly considered the Gospel to be the foundation stone of the Order of Friars Minor! In still other passages of his chronicle he reports that, in accordance with the Gospel, the brothers used the greeting of peace and enjoyed the freedom of eating and drinking.[22]

This last element, though in restricted form, along with such evangelical practices as begging pardon for offenses committed and the non-taking of oaths, is listed also by Thomas of Eccleston. The brothers, writes Thomas, "should not eat among seculars, except for three morsls of meat for the sake of *observances of the Gospel,* because the rumor had come to him [Francis] that the brothers were eating avidly. . . . There also grew up among them the very religious custom never to swear to anything but simply to say, 'Know that it is so.' As soon as any of them was reprimanded either by a superior or by a confrere, he would immediately answer, *'Mea culpa,* I am at fault,' and frequently he would even prostrate himself."[23]

Hugh of Digne is a particularly fascinating source for he clearly recaptured the enthusiasm for the Gospel found in the earlier sources. He explained, for example, that the friars' rule itself is evangelical, a thought later echoed by Jordan of Giano. By this Hugh meant that the rule of the Friars Minor is the same one which the apostles gave to the early Church and which was later adopted by various founders of religious life. He goes so far as to maintain that the rule of the friars embodies the totality of Gospel perfection.[24]

By so doing Hugh repeated a thought already found in Thomas of Celano, namely that observance of the Rule is equivalent to observance of the Gospel.[25] A very similar claim, it will be recalled, was made before the curia by Cardinal John of St. Paul in behalf of Francis' unwritten Rule. "We must be careful," the Cardinal warned his collegues. "If we refuse this beggarman's request because it is new or too difficult, we may be sinning against *Christ's Gospel,* because he is only asking us to approve *a form of Gospel life.* Anyone who says that a vow *to live according to the perfection of the Gospel* contains something new or unreasonable or too difficult to be observed, is guilty of blasphemy against Christ, the Author of the Gospel."[26]

What is even more significant about Hugh, however, is that he seems to have borrowed almost verbatim the opinion of Rupert of Deutz (d. 1130), who taught that the Rule of St. Benedict was in perfect accord with Gospel perfection.[27] Hugh extended Rupert's equation one step further to read thus: the apostolic rule = the rule of the Friars Minor.

The sole concern of the first friars, maintained Hugh, was to observe the Gospel. Instead of riding horseback, they walked from place to place like Christ. They used the greeting of peace; when one town did not receive them, they fled to another; they ate and drank what was placed before them. They kept their speech simple and refrained from taking oaths; they avoided using titles of honor, such as "Master" and "Lord." They quickly begged pardon for offences; they did not litigate in courts of law, nor resist evil done to them. They wore poor clothing, went about barefoot, lived in perfect harmony and made no provision for the future. They were poor in spirit, gentle, merciful and peace-loving.[28]

Some of these elements, it is important to note, were not mentioned in any other source. By listing so many "evangelical" elements, Hugh perhaps wished to paint a stylized portrait of the early friars' life-style based completely on the Gospels, in much the same way that certain passages of the Acts of the Apostles (2: 44 ff.; 4: 32-35) summarized and preserved the ideals of the early Christians.

Reviewing the above paragraphs, one quickly notices that the concept of "Gospel life" is to an extent a fluid reality; that is, its contents change somewhat from source to source. This is so because none of these early sources intended to define or to give a systematic account of this or of any other fundamental value. Rather, each source, so to speak, chose pebbles of various sizes and colors and out of these—depending on the purpose and needs each writing was intended to fill—it constructed its own individualized mosaic. By adding, eliminating or shading the various evangelical elements, one author created a very rich mosaic, while another was satisfied with only a sketchy version.

* * * *

When one compares the Gospel life of the Friars Minor

as described above with the ideals of their predeccessors, there emerge certain important parallels. For example, the basic message which Peter Damian (1007–72), the great reformer of the Church, offered his hearers, namely penance and the conversion of one's heart to God, was also the core of St. Francis' teaching. Peter stressed the Gospel ideals he discovered in Matthew and Luke, particularly the Sermon on the Mount (Mt 5–7), Christ's invitation to the young man (Mt 19:21) and the need of carrying one's cross (Lk 9:23).[29]

An even closer parallel to St. Francis' Gospel teachings is provided by Stephan of Thiers-Muret, who placed his full reliance on the Gospels. Stephan taught that the sole norm for all Christiams, as well as the only true and ultimate basis for life in religion was the Rule of Rules, that is, the Gospel.[30]

Moreover, the phrase which a biographer applied to Stephan, namely "he was no deaf hearer of the Gospel,"[31] is the same which Celano used in reference to Francis.[32] It is noteworthy, too, that an English friar knew of Stephan and frequently repeated the advice he gave to his followers, namely that they should avoid contact with lay people.[33] In view of this evidence, one is led to ask whether it is not possible for the early franciscan community to have been acquainted with other elements of Stephan's teaching as well, for example his great dependence on the Gospels.

Though the above points of contact between Francis and his predecessors are meaningful, they nonetheless reveal only a similarity of *teaching* and not of *life-style*, since both Peter Damian and Stephan were representatives of more or less traditional monasticism. The itinerant preachers of France, however, do offer significant parallels with Francis' day to day style of living. These men, as their biographers clearly indicate, were eager to follow the Gospel demands so literally, that they renounced all their possessions and went about from place to place proclaiming the Kingdom of God and encouraging their hearers to free their hearts from slavery to perishable values. Thus a man like Robert of Arbrissel, the unshod, bearded, and roughly-dressed preacher of penance who went about the countryside without staff or purse,[34] can be considered a true precursor of St. Francis.

Even more to the point is the example of Norbert of Gennep who observed this demand of the Gospel in a literal fashion: "He carried neither money, purse, nor shoes, nor two tunics, but was content with a few books and vestments for Mass."[35] Norbert and his followers were so concerned about living the Gospel that the phrase "according to the Gospel of Christ" was later added to the formula of profession of the Premonstratensian Order.[36] Such literal observance of the Gospels, combined with a deep desire to lead this life in perfect fidelity to the Church, are two important points of contact between the itinerant preachers of the twelfth century and St. Francis and his followers.

The apostolic lay-movements of the late twelfth and early thirteenth centuries also provide significant parallels with the early franciscan community. For example, the Gospel words, "No one can serve two masters, God and mammon" (Mt 6:24), which played a key role in the conversion of Peter Waldo,[37] are precisely the words which Richerius Senonensis has St. Francis tell his father upon his own conversion.[38] Waldo's desire to live without possessing gold or silver and without concern for the morrow,[39] clearly reflects St. Francis' own way of life. In fact the latter element, repeated later by the Poor Catholics,[40] is listed by the Four Masters, Hugh of Digne, and some minor sources as elements of the friars' own Gospel way of life. Furthermore, the ideal which Waldo presented to the Pope, namely "to live wholly according to the doctrine of the Gospel and to observe it to the letter perfectly,"[41] summarizes St. Francis own basic desire beautifully. Indeed, Francis and Waldo were one in considering the Gospel as the absolute norm of life and doctrine for *all* Christians.

Because of these similarities it is not unreasonable to ask whether Francis was aquainted with and perhaps even influenced by Waldo's ideals. There seems to be enough historical plausibility to warrant a positive answer. The young Francis, for example, could have heard about the Waldenses and similar apostolic groups from his own father who frequently took business trips to Southern France.[42] It is possible, too, that the priest at Portiuncula whom Francis approached for an explanation of the Gospel was a member of the Waldenses. This seems to be borne out by the interpretation he gave to Francis. The sources, moreover, relate that when Francis begged or spoke of his *poor* life, he often used the French language. This led K. Esser to pose the following fascinating question, "whether Francis was not thereby using the formulas of the Waldenses?"[43] Finally, it is interesting to note that the Waldenses begged alms "for the love of God." Francis, one recalls, never denied alms to people who begged using this formula.[44]

Real as these similarities are, it is a fact that Waldo and Francis, and consequently their followers, differed in some important respects. The followers of Waldo, for example, considered lying and killing as always gravely sinful and doubted the efficacy of prayers for the dead.[45] These elements played no role in the franciscan community. The Waldenses forbade all swearing of oaths, a demand which was also observed, though in a modified form, by the Humiliati.[46] Among the franciscan sources, this element is mentioned only by Thomas of Eccleston, Hugh of Digne and Pope Honorius.[47]

Instead of forbidding oaths, St. Francis rather encouraged

his followers to keep their speech simple and chaste, and not to contend in words. The *perfecti* among the Waldenses, moreover, were not allowed to work but were to depend on alms from their benefactors. In this respect, too, the friars were more akin to the Humiliati and to Bernard Primus, who encouraged manual work among their members. St. Francis, the early legends, and Jacques de Vitry testify to the fact that manual work was taken for granted among the first friars. The fundamental defference between the two movements, however, was their relationship to the Church. St. Francis was always most concerned that his sons remain obdient and subject to Church authority.

The fundamental ideal of the Humiliati, namely, "to live according to the letter of the Gospel and like the apostles to preach to the people the truths of salvation,"[48] also reflects the desire of St. Francis and his followers. Moreover, the *propositum* of their Third Order, that is, a short summary of their ideals based on the words of Scripture, reminds one of the primitive rule which St. Francis presented to Pope Innocent.[49] In this connection it is not wholly irrelevant to recall that Celano also referred to the Rule of St. Francis as *propositum conversationis*,[50] a technical term for "rule of life," which also applied to the Poor Catholics and to the community of Bernard Primus.

Other elements of the life style of these latter two groups such as observing the evangelical counsels as commands, reciting the Our Father, fasting only on days prescribed by the common law of the Church, wearing a simple habit, and promising to live in obedience to the pope and clergy,[51] were also observed by the Friars Minor. In addition, the followers of Bernard Primus were to avoid "suspicious dealings with women,"[52] an element found also in the Rule of 1223. What is interesting however, is that none of these apostolic groups lists the salutation of peace and the evangelical freedom of eating and drinking as part of their life style; these elements, it will be recalled, were observed by the early friars, as so many of the sources testify.

As in the case of Waldo, so, too, here one might pose the question whether Francis could have been acquainted with or even influenced by these latter groups. Unfortunately there is no firm historical evidence to warrant such a claim. Yet it is fascinating to consider that precisely duing the formative years of the franciscan community, that is, during the first decade of the thirteenth century, a number of groups, originating in Southern France and Northern Italy, travelled through the Italian countryside on their way to Rome to receive approbation for their form of life and then made the journey northward to return home.

The leaders of the Humiliati, for example, came to Rome in 1199 and received approval in 1201. Durandus of Huesca came in 1208, while Bernard Primus arrived in 1210. Perhaps news of these pilgrims travelling to and from Rome filtered to Assisi and even reached Francis' own ears. These groups, after all, would have been eager to broadcast their own ideals, as well as their success in Rome. Francis, moreover, could also have come into contact with these or similar groups during his own travels and visits to Rome in 1206 and 1210.

The case for an indirect influence is more persuasive. It seems quite likely that the form of life which the pope and curia approved for these earlier groups served as a model for approving and moulding the mendicant orders some years later. Thus, St. Dominic and his preachers, a clerical order dedicated to fighting heresy by observing evangelical poverty and fostering theological study, may have been modelled on Durandus and the Poor Catholics. And because St. Francis and his followers sought primarily to incarnate the life of the Gospels, a life which revolved about personal conversion, poverty, humility, charitable works and preaching, they could have been modeled on Bernard Primus and his community.[53]

What is even more fascinating is the convincing argumentation proposed by K. Esser to show that St. Francis came into contact with representatives of the Albigensian or Catharist heresy.[54] Not only was his diocese a center for these heretics, points out Esser, but the very town of Assisi elected one of their number as mayor in 1203. Francis, then a wide-awake young man of twenty-one, must have followed these religious and political developments with great interest. Very likely, too, Francis was acquainted with the decrees of the Lateran Council, some of which were directed specifically against this sect.

It is all but certain that Francis came into direct contact with the Cathari in Northern Italy during his preaching journey.[55] Finally, it is not altogether insignificant that John of St. Paul, the cardinal who presented Francis and his rule of life to the curia, was a papal legate to an Albigensian territory in 1200/01.[56] May one not conclude that the cardinal was personally acquainted with the danger which this heretical poverty movement, in control of fifteen hundred towns and cities, presented to the Church and therefore desired that the curia approve Francis' petition in order to offset the sect's influence?

Bearing in mind these probable contacts which St. Francis had with the Cathari and their teachings, one is better able to understand why the saint goes out of his way to stress over and over certain aspects of doctrine, for example that God *alone* is true God, *alone* holy, *alone* kind, *alone* almighty, that God has given man his *whole* body, his *whole* soul and *all* his life, that Jesus was born of Mary's womb and shed *thick drops of blood* during his passion.[57] This emphasis by Francis on certain doctrines and words shows that he was reacting consciously to the teachings of the Cathari and the Albigenses, who believed in two supreme principles, considered that matter and flesh were created by the evil god, and viewed Christ as an angel who appeared on earth in only the appearance of a human body.[58]

* * * *

The above reflections clearly point out how much a man of his time Francis really was and how willingly he let himself be swept off his feet by the envigorating breeze of renewal in his day. Yet this is not the whole story, for there is a scintillating facet in the career of St. Francis which clearly separates him from practically all other contemporary *pauperes Christi*. True, the various apostolic groups revived a number of important Christian values. But they did so by concentrating their attention almost exclusively on only one facet of the Gospel, namely Christ's "missionary" discourse to his apostles. Thus these enthusiastic Christians went about the countryside barefoot and bearded, carrying no money and wearing only ragged clothing, in order to preach penance.

Francis also began his evangelical *metanoia* by observing these demands, as his biographers emphasize.[59] But during the course of his life this evangelical seed blossomed into the observance of the *whole* Gospel. This dramatic widening of evangelical horizons becomes crystal-clear to the reader who patiently examines the numerous Gospel citations in the saint's writings, as well as the deeply biblical themes found in his admonitions and in the Rule of 1221.[60] This is also the thrust of the words he wrote in his last days, a summary so to speak, of what his whole life was all about: ". . . the Most High himself made it clear to me that I must live *the life of the Gospel*" (Testament; Omn, 68).

What we have here is a deep-seated conviction on the part of Francis that he was called to live not simply a *part* of the Gospel, say for example the missionary discourse, but rather the Gospel of Jesus Christ as such, whole and entire. For Francis such an observance of the Gospel revolved about the great Commandment of Love of God and neighbor, a love which embraced all the characteristics and ramifications listed by the Apostle Paul (1 Cor 13).

Because of this love operating in his life, Francis was gentle and patient with others, even with the wayward and the lax. He castigated and upbraided no one; he labelled no one a sinner. This was a truly and wholly Christian attitude, one which was far more "evangelical" than the usual arrogance and holier-than-thou attitude of many individuals who in their enthusiasm for the "apostolic" life never grew beyond the literal and oftentimes petty observance of the missionary discourse!

The difference which K. Esser noted between Francis and the Cathari can also be applied to many other "apostles" of the twelfth and thirteenth centuries: "In the final analysis what the Cathari lacked was an abundant, true love. And this love Francis gave to his age: love of God, love of the God-Man Jesus Christ, love of his mother; love for Christ's work of salvation, love of his incarnation, Passion and Eucharist; love for the Church and for all men, even for sinners and unbelievers. Before the radiance of this love, darkness disappeared."[61]

Notes

1. *Vita s. Francisci,* 16 (AnalFranc X, 342).

2. *Legenda chori,* 4 (AnalFranc X, 120).

3. For Francis the words "rule" and "life" are quite synonymous. This is clearly evident in the opening words of the Rule of 1223: "The *Rule* and *life* of the Friars Minor is this. . ." (Omn, 57.)

4. See *Testament* (Omn, 67-69) and *Rule of 1223,* ch. 1-6 (Omn, 57-61.)

5. See K. Esser, "Sancta mater ecclesia romana. Die Kirchenfrommigkeit des hl. Franziskus von Assisi," in WissWeish, 24(1961), 11.

6. *Vita s. Francisci,* 15 (AnalFranc X, 324).

7. Leg 3 Comp, 25 (Omn, 915).

8. *Chronica de gestis regum Angliae* (TestMin, 23). See also Bartholomaus of Trient, *Liber epilogorum in gesta Sanctorum (Test-*Min, 64); *Legenda Monacensis,* 8 (AnalFranc X, 697).

9. See 2 Celano, 4 (Omn, 364).

10. See *Legend of Perugia,* 44 (Omn, 1022-24).

11. See *Ascendit ad nos* (BullFr, 41); *Coelestis altitudo* (BullFr, 93-96); *Receptis affectione* (BullFr, 203); *Considerentes olim* (BullFr, 233-34).

12. See *Cronica* (Scalia, pp. 106, 698, 297, 302, 467).

13. 1 Celano, 51 (Omn, 272); 2 Celano, 78 (Omn, 428).

14. *Chronicon* (TestMin, 17 f.).

15. *Chronicon* (TestMin, 20).

16. *Historia Orientalis* (Omn, 1611).

17. See Leg 3 Comp, 43,57.

18. *Testament of St. Clare,* 10 (Brady, p. 84).

19. Four Masters, ch. 1, 3, 4 (Oliger, pp. 125, 140, 147).

20. *Chronicle,* 2 (Hermann, p. 21).

21. *Chronicle,* 16 (Hermann, p. 32).

22. *Chronicle,* 14, 12 (Hermann pp. 29, 27).

23. Thomas of Eccleston, *Chronicle,* 5 (Hermann, pp. 117-18).

24. *Commentary on the Rule,* ch. 1 (fol. 3v).

25. *Legenda chori,* 5 (AnalFranc X, 121); 1 Celano, 32 (Omn, 254); 2 Celano, 62, 216 (Omn, 415, 535).

26. St. Bonaventure, *Major Life of St. Francis,* III, 9 (Omn, 652).

27. See Rupert of Deutz, *De vita vere apostolica,* IV (PL 170, 653).

28. *Commentary on the Rule,* ch. 1 (fol. 3v-4r).

29. See for example *Sermo 18* (PL 144, 609).

30. *Regula s. Stephani* (PL 204, 1136, 1138).

31. *Vita s. Stephani* (PL 204, 1008).

32. 1 Celano, 22 (Omn, 247). Very likely is Sulpicius Severus, *De vita s. Martini,* 2, (PL 20, 162), the common source of both these references.

33. Thomas of Eccleston, *Chronicle,* 14 (Hermann, p. 173-74).

34. See *Vita b. Roberti de Arbrissello* (PL 162, 1052).

35. *Vita Norberti* (MGSS, XII, 675).

36. Adam Praemonstratensis, *Liber de ordine, habitu et professione canonicorum Ordinis Praemonstratensis, Sermo 8,* 2 (PL 198, 508 f.).

37. *Chronicon universale anonymi Laudunensis* (MGSS, XXVI, 448).

38. *Gesta Senonesis ecclesiae* (TestMin, 32).

39. *Chronicon universale* (MGSS, XXVI, 449).

40. *Propositum des Pauvres Catholiques (1208),* ch. 2, in G. G.

Meersseman, *Dossier de l'Ordre de la Penitence au XIIIe Siecle* (Fribourg, 1961), p. 283.

41. Herbert Grundmann, *Religiose Bewegungen im Mittelalter* (Darmstadt: Wissenschaftliche Buchgesellschaft, 1961), p. 59 n. 107.

42. See Paul Sabatier, *Vie de S. Francois d'Assise* (Paris, 1931), 9f.

43. K. Esser "Die religiosen Bewegungen des Hochmittelalters," in *Festabe Joseph Lortz* (Baden-Baden, 1958), II, 299.

44. See J. B. Pierron, *Die Katholischen Armen* (Freiburg, 1911), p. 172; 1 Celano, 17; 2 Celano, 5, 196.

45. See Grundmann, p. 96.

46. See *Chronicon universale* (MGSS, XXVI, 449 f.).

47. *Nuper nobis* (BullFr, 21).

48. Pierron, p. 14.

49. Ibid., p. 16.

50. See 2 Celano, 16; Grundmann, p. 133.

51. Meersseman, p. 283.

52. *Ne quis* (PL 216, 649).

53. Grundmann, p. 123; Pierron, pp. 135–60.

54. Kajetan Esser, "Der hl. Franziskus und die religiosen Bewegungen seiner Zeit," in *San Francisco nella ricerca storica degli ultimi ottanta anni* (Convegni del centro di studi sulla spiritualita medievale IX: Todi, 1971), pp. 108-20.

55. 2 Celano, 78-9 (Omn, 427-28); Stephan of Bourbon, *Anecdotes historiques,* ed. Lecoy de la Marche (Omn, 1605-6).

56. Grundmann, p. 130

57. See *Rule of 1221,* ch. 23 (Omn, 52); *Letter to the Faithful* (Omn, 93). In some cases the English translation fails to bring out this emphasis.

58. Esser, "Der hl. Franziskus und die religiosen Bewegungen," pp. 108-20.

59. See, for example, 1 Celano, 22 (Omn, 246-47).

60. The number of biblical citations in the writings of St. Francis is truly amazing. See E. D'Oisy, "Saint Francois d'Assise: La Bible et le Saint Evangile," in EtudFranc, 23 (1927), 498-529, 646-56; 24 (1928), 68-80.

61. Kajetan Esser, "Franziskus von Assisi und die Katharer seiner Zeit," in ArchFrancHist, 51 (1958), 264.

3.

THE FOLLOWING
OF
CHRIST

Another key aspect of the friars' way of life is very aptly summarized in the oft-repeated phrase, "to follow in the footsteps of Christ." To understand precisely what this theme meant to the early franciscan community, it is very helpful to examine first of all the image of Christ which the sources contain.

1. A Specialized Image of Christ

At the inspiration of the Lord, St. Francis was led, as we have seen, *to live* according to the form of the holy Gospels. But this same inspiration of the Lord also led Francis *to read* the Gospels continually and *to mediate* deeply on the events of Christ's life therein reported. This fact is attested to by a certain brother, who, seeing Francis in great pain, encouraged him to seek consolation in the written Word of God with these words: "Father, you have *always sought refuge in the Scriptures,* and they have always given you remedies for your pains. I pray you to have something *read* to you now from the prophets; perhaps your spirit will rejoice in the Lord." Francis' response to this suggestion clearly indicates that the sacred book was his life-long companion. "It is good to read the testimonies of Scripture; it is good to seek the Lord our God in them," Francis tells the brother. "As for me, however, *I have already made so much of Scripture my own* that I have more than enough to meditate on and revolve in my mind" (2 Celano, 105; Omn, 448).

And what did Francis discover in the pages of Scripture? Without doubt, the person of Jesus Christ and a description of his earthly life: his humble birth in a lowly stable, his preaching and miracles, his concern for the poor, his horrible passion and cruel death on the cross. These vivid images and scenes must have fired Francis' poetic imagination and his constant meditation on them led him to form a very personalized image of Christ in his mind and heart. Thus in his *Letter to the Faithful,* Francis contemplates with loving admiration the "Word of the Father," who was "rich beyond measure," but nonetheless emptied himself of all glory and "took on our weak human nature" (Omn, 93). During his life on earth this "Son of the living, all-powerful God" lived like a pilgrim and stranger, with "no home of his own," and was not ashamed to depend "on alms" (Rule of 1221, ch. 9; Omn, 39).

It is the Christ of Gethsemane, however, who holds a special place in Francis' heart. It was then that Christ "prayed to his Father, too, saying, 'Father, if it is possible, let this cup pass away from me" (Mt 26:39); and his sweat fell to the ground like thick drops of blood (Lk 22:44). Yet he bowed to his Father's will and said, 'Father, thy will be done; yet not as I will, but as thou willest'" (Mt 26:42, 39) (Omn, 93). This complete surrender of his will into the hands of his Father, Francis points out in the sixth Admonition, led Christ, the "Good Shepherd," to endure "the agony of the cross" (Omn, 81).

This same Jesus Christ who humbled himself at the Incarnation, "when he came from his heavenly throne," continues to do so *every day,* Francis emphasizes in his first Admonition, for he "comes to us and lets us see him in *abjection,* when he descends from the bosom of the Father into the hands of the priest at the altar" (Omn, 78). What is significant about this text is that Francis saw the *kenosis,* the self-emptying of Christ, taking place not only at his birth and during his earthly life, but even more especially in the Eucharist. In fact Francis cannot contain his wonder when he comtemplates Christ's continued presence among us in such humility. "Our whole being should be seized with fear," he writes in his *Letter to a Chapter* like the poet he is, "the whole world should tremble and heaven rejoice, when Christ the Son of the living God is present on the altar in the hands of the priest. What wonderful majesty! That the Lord of the whole universe, God and the Son of God, should *humble* himself like this and *hide* under the form of a little bread, for our salvation" (Omn 105).

Of course Francis came to this particular image of Christ, that is, of the humble Christ who lived in poverty and who suffered and died on the Cross, not merely because he read the Gospels, but because he already had a personal encounter with the poor, suffering Christ. This took place in the church of San Damiano, when the Crucified Christ spoke to the young Francis. "From then on," Thomas of Celano reports, "*compassion* for the crucified was *rooted in his holy soul. . . .* And from then on he could never keep himself from *weeping,* even *bewailing* in a loud voice *the passion of Christ* which was always, as it were, before his mind. He filled the ways with his sighs" (2 Celano, 10–11; Omn, 370–1). This vivid experience of the Crucified certainly predisposed Francis to discover and to emphasize the image of the poor, suffering Christ when he began to read and to meditate on the Gospels.

The other sources relating to the early franciscan community present much the same image of Christ as contained in the writings of St. Francis. In his first biography of Francis, Thomas of Celano states that what particularly impressed the saint about Christ was the humility he displayed at the Incarnation and the love for mankind which led him to suffer and die on the cross (n. 84–85; Omn, 299–300). Once, when Francis saw a little lamb "going along and feeding humbly and quietly," he was inwardly touched with sorrow and immediately thought of Jesus Christ who "walked in the same way *meekly* and *humbly* among the pharisees and chief priests" (n. 77; Omn, 293-94). In the second bi-ography, Celano has Francis address these words to his brothers: "Dearest brothers, the Son of God was more noble than we and *he made himself poor* for us in this world" (n. 74; Omn, 425). Again, it is the *kenotic* Christ who is here dominant in the mind of Francis.

Julian of Speyer, too, emphasizes the profound love which Francis had for the poor, crucified Christ.[i] Much more vividly does the author of the *Sacrum Commercium* portray the intimate and lasting relationship between Christ and poverty. "Certainly, at his birth you [poverty] met him [Christ] in all fidelity, so that in you he might find a place that would suit him, and not in earthly delights. He was laid in a manger, says the evangelist, because there was no room for him in the inn. And thus, always inseparable from him, you accompanied him so that throughout his life . . . though the foxes had dens and the birds of the air nests, he nevertheless had nowhere to lay his head" (n. 19; Omn, 1562).

The image of the humble, poor and suffering, but also loving Savior was deeply impressed on the heart of St. Clare. In a letter to Agnes of Prague, Clare shared this image of Christ which was ever before her eyes. She encouraged Agnes to look constantly into the "mirror" of Christ's life and there to discover the essence of the Christian life. "Behold, I say," Clare writes, "the beginning of this mirror: the *poverty* of Him Who was placed in the manger and wrapped in swaddling clothes. O marvelous *humility!* O astounding *poverty!* The King of the angels, the Lord of heaven and earth, is laid in a manger! In the middle of the mirror consider the *humility,* the blessed *poverty,* the untold *labors* and *burdens* which He sustained for the redemption of the human race. In the end of that mirror contemplate the unspeakable *charity* with which He willed to *suffer* on

the tree of the Cross and to die thereon the most shameful
kind of death." By contemplating this image of Christ,
Clare told Agnes, she will be "set afire with love ever more
strongly" for her Lord and Savior.[2]

In like manner, Hugh of Digne[3] and the papal documents[4]
place great emphasis on the poor Christ. Even the worldly
Salimbene underscored this same image in the pages of his
chronicle. In a dream, which helped the troubled Salimbene
to realize a fundamental characteristic of the Franciscan Order, he met Jesus, Mary and Joseph, as they went about
begging for alms from door to door. Jesus turned to Salimbene and spoke these words to him: "I am your Savior
. . . I am he who left his home, gave up his inheritance
and delivered his very life into the hands of his enemies for
the salvation of mankind. So do not be ashamed, my son,
to go begging out of love for me, so that you, too, can
say in all truth what is written, 'I am indeed a beggar and
am poor, but God provides for me.'"[5]

Jacques de Vitry, too, reminded the friars, in a sermon he
preached to them, of the Christ who "emptied" himself of
glory and became a "slave" by exchanging his eternal riches
for a life of poverty and hardship" (Phil 2:6,7).[6] And it is
this same image of Christ which Bonaventure incorporated
into his spiritual theology: "In order to give us an example,
Christ became not only a poor man and a beggar, but became even naked and totally despised, that he might give
an example how to despise the world perfectly."[7]

* * * *

The above image of Christ so uniformly proclaimed by
the franciscan sources, has been labelled "specialized." By
this is meant that these sources stress only certain aspects
of Christ, primarily his humility, poverty and suffering,

while omitting other aspects presented in the Gospels and emphasized in the earlier centuries of the Church. Thus, the franciscan image of Christ is markedly different from that which was cultivated in the art and piety of the pre-Constantinian Church.

In those early centuries the Christian people looked to Christ as the Savior and the Good Shepherd. They looked to him as the bringer of salvation. Often, too, they viewed him as the new Orpheus and as the Pilot who steered the ship of the Church. In the fourth century, following Constantine's victory over paganism, the image of Christ in the mind of Christians began to change. They now stressed Christ as the Victor crowned by God, as the glorious Creator enthroned in heaven, as the victorious Emperor and Ruler.[8] The franciscan view of Christ examined above is not immediately related to these images. What is important to note in this short survey is the influence which social, political and cultural factors exerted on contemporary piety. In particular, these factors help mold the kind of image of Christ the faithful cultivate during any given age. This same dynamic relationship between culture and piety is noticeable throughout the centuries.

At the same time it must be pointed out that the franciscan image of Christ is by no means an absolutely new creation. After all, the image of the poor Christ and the consequent "following" and "imitation" of Christ by carrying one's cross and by living in poverty was already a vibrant reality among the Eastern Fathers, for example Clement of Alexandria and Origen, among the founders of monasticism, such as Anthony and Pachomius, and finally among the Latin Fathers, such as Tertullian, Augustine, Jerome, Cassian, and Isidore of Seville.[9]

More proximately, however, the franciscan image of Christ was influenced by and grounded in the religious and social movements of the eleventh and twelfth centuries. The fresh interest in the Sacred Scriptures which flourished during these years, combined with the crusaders' efforts to liberate the Holy Land, resulted in a heightened consciousness of Christ's humanity and his life on earth. The human side of the life of Christ was thus brought closer to the religious life and experience of the *individual* Christian. And soon a new image of Christ was born in the minds of Christians: the Christ who was poor and lowly, who trod the dusty paths of Palestine, the Christ who preached to the people, but particularly to the poor, the Christ who became the servant of all, the Christ who loved and accepted the weak and the sick, the Christ who went in search of each sinner, and the Christ who suffered terribly and who died a hideous death for all mankind, but also *for each individual.*[10]

Peter Damian was one who helped popularize this new image of Christ. He declared that the entire life of Jesus and not merely his preaching gave the Christian a pattern to follow. By passing to the Father by way of the cross, Peter Damian declared, Christ indicated the *transitus* which each Christian must undergo. Henceforth each disciple of Christ must follow the Master by carrying his own cross.[11] Hugh of St. Victor taught a very similar doctrine. The Canon Regular, he stated, was to look for inspiration to the Christ who gave up his glory and associated himself with the poor of this earth. It is for the sake of Christ, therefore, that the Canon Regular is to become poor.[12] The biographer of Stephen of Thiers-Muret, too, emphasized that he did not wish to own anything, because he wanted to imitate "the footsteps of his Redeemer."[13]

The itinerant preachers of France, who renounced all their possessions and went from place to place to proclaim the Kingdom of God were very successful in popularizing the image of the poor Christ. The ideal of Robert of Arbrissel, for example, was expressed in these striking words: "nude, to follow the nude Christ on the cross."[14] In like manner, Bernard of Thiron exhorted his followers from his deathbed to imitate the poor, crucified Christ.[15] Bernard of Clairvaux continued this same tradition by stressing the poverty and humility of the earthly life of Jesus. Christ, born to poor parents in a lowly stable during the cold of winter and the darkness of night and visited by poor shepherds, was for him a vivid reality.[16]

No doubt, all these influences helped to mold the franciscan image of the poor, suffering Christ. In the final analysis, however, this image was refined and rekindled by St. Francis' own religious genius, that is, by his own constant meditation on the Gospels and by the tangible experience of the Crucified Christ in his own life.

2. To Follow in the Footsteps of Christ

The "following" of Christ, as it is described in the early franciscan sources, is the natural and logical consequence of the kind of image of Christ which Francis and his brothers bore in their hearts.

Francis' own writings indicate how deeply he grounded his teaching concerning the following of Christ on the doctrine of the New Testament. The Father lives in "unapproachable light" (1 Tm 6:16), declares Francis, and "no one has ever seen God" (Jn 1:18). But Jesus, God's very Son, by becoming a man like us, has made God visible and accessible. Therefore, whoever knows Jesus Christ, knows the Father also; and whoever sees Jesus Christ, sees also the Father. Indeed, it is only through Jesus Christ that one can go to the Father, for Jesus is "the way, the truth and the life" (Jn 14:6-9).[17]

Since Jesus Christ is man's way to the Father and since

Francis wanted to "return" to the Father, he focused his attention very earnestly on the person of Jesus Christ, with a view to following in his very "footsteps." What particularly struck Francis about Christ, as was pointed out above, was his intimate relationship with and loving surrender to the heavenly Father. For this reason Francis wanted himself and his brothers to enter into a relationship of love with the Father and to surrender themselves wholly to him.[18] "We must *love God*," Francis exclaims, "and *adore him* with a pure heart and mind, because *this is what he seeks above all else.* . . . "[19] Such love and adoration of God, in turn, will establish "a *dwelling-place within ourselves* where he can stay, he who is the Lord God almighty, Father, Son, and Holy Spirit."[20] A man who is growing in this relationship with the Lord will "let go" completely of his "old self"; he will not "claim" any good as his own, but will ascribe to the Lord whatever good "God says or does in him."[21]

St. Francis was likewise deeply impressed by the fact that Jesus was a man of such deep love, that he even loved and forgave his traitor Judas.[22] Thus, Francis wanted to "follow" Christ by also becoming a man of love; he emphasized the Golden Rule of love of neighbor[23] and encouraged his brothers to love each other with the tenderness of a mother.[24]

But Francis saw clearly that Christ's attitudes of heart were expressed externally in a life of voluntary poverty and humility. Hence he wanted his brothers to live in the same way. Because they wanted to "follow Christ," they were to sell all their possessions and give to the poor; they were to wear only rough clothing; in times of necessity they were even to go begging without being ashamed, because Christ himself was not ashamed to live from alms. The image of the poor Christ is certainly present in this passage of the Rule of 1223: "The friars are to appropriate nothing for themselves, neither a house, nor a place, nor anything else.

As 'strangers and pilgrims' (1 Pt 2:11) in this world, who serve God in poverty and humility, they should beg alms trustingly. And there is no reason why they should be ashamed, because God made himself poor for us in this world" (ch. 6; Omn, 61). It is by "following" Christ, by taking on his attitudes and life-style, ultimately by becoming Christ-like, that Francis wished to make his way to the Father.

The "following" of the poor, humble, suffering Christ is even more dramatically recorded in 1 Celano. On his death-bed, St. Francis, whom Celano calls the "crucified servant of the crucified Christ," lay naked on a floor and was covered with ashes, while his brothers read the story of the Lord's Passion (n. 110; Omn, 324). Such was the depth of St. Francis' following of Christ: an internal emptying of self and a complete surrender to the Lord, combined with an external surrender of all material goods and values. Jacques de Vitry applies this ideal to the Order at large. The friars, he says, "follow" Christ who "emptied" himself of glory and became a slave. Because of this "following," he calls the friars "the true poor men of the Crucified One."[25]

A number of the sources seem to lose sight of the internal dimension of the following of Christ and concentrate their attention on its ascetical aspect, particularly on the external practice of poverty. Buoncompagni, writing about 1220, stated that the friars "follow" Christ, because they go about barefoot and wear hairshirts.[26] Julian of Speyer reflects this same view when he says that St. Francis achieved a high degree of conformity with the "poor, Crucified Christ" by living in voluntary poverty. For St. Clare, life on this earth consisted in following Christ, that is, in taking up one's cross and observing the highest poverty. Thomas of Celano summarizes Clare's life and desire thus: "She strove by *perfect poverty* to be made like the Poor Crucified, that no

passing thing of earth might separate the lover from the Beloved or hinder the course of her union with God."[27]

Salimbene's dream of the begging Christ convinced him
that the friars were an Order of *poor men;* they were to follow Christ by possessing nothing whatever and by depending completely on the providence of God.[28] In like manner
Hugh of Digne stated that the friars are to "imitate" Christ
and the apostles; by this he meant that they are to conform
themselves to the poor, naked Christ who went about begging
for alms.[29]

The papal documents, too, declared that all the followers
of St. Francis are to serve the poor Christ by living in poverty. The friars are to "put on" the naked Christ. Indeed,
by living in poverty, they make the life of Christ "manifest"
in themselves. These are the striking words which Pope
Gregory IX addressed to the friars: ". . . by bearing within your hearts the mortification of Christ, *so that the life of
Jesus may be manifest in you,* you have embraced the glory
of true humility."[30] Life in poverty and humility is meant
to transform the inner man into Christ!

Several of the sources just examined emphasized the role
which poverty plays in the "following" of Christ. This is
not to say that the franciscan tradition limits this theme
to the practice of poverty. Three of the sources approach
the following of Christ from a significantly different perspective and thus reveal how rich and many-sided this concept really is for the early friars.

Brother Elias, for example, stressed the deeply biblical
meaning of the following of Christ, that is, carrying out the
work which Christ performed while on earth. According to
Elias, Francis was a "light," which the heavenly Father
sent to man. Just like Christ, so, too, did Francis preach
the Kingdom of God and fashioned for the Lord a "new
people." Francis also suffered, died, and entered into life.

He "ascended" to the father, was glorified in heaven, and now intercedes for his followers who are still on earth. According to Elias, Francis "followed" Christ in the sense that he "re-capitulated" Christ's entire *life* on earth, as well as his transitus to the Father: Christ's origin and public life, his passion and death, his ascension and glorification! The wounds of Christ which Francis bore in his body, so that he himself appeared "crucified," were a striking sign and proof that Francis attained the height of evangelical perfection.[31]

In 1 Celano, on the other hand, the theme of following in the footsteps of Christ is often intimately connected with interior devotion. When Thomas of Celano writes that Francis "followed in the footsteps of Christ" he sometimes means that the saint *meditated* on the words and deeds of the Lord recorded in the Gospels and made these events present to his mind. Francis "would *recall* Christ's words through persistent *meditation* and bring to *mind* his deeds through the most penetrating *consideration.* The humility of the incarnation and charity of the passion occupied his *memory* particularly, to the extent that he wanted to *think* of hardly anything else" (n. 84; Omn, 299).

Celano goes out of his way to emphasize that Francis often "followed" his Lord in this way: "Indeed, he was *always occupied* with Jesus; Jesus he bore in his heart, Jesus in his mouth, Jesus in his ears, Jesus in his eyes, Jesus in his hands, Jesus in the rest of his members. O how often, when he sat down to eat, *hearing* or *speaking* or *thinking* of Jesus, he forgot bodily food. . . . Indeed, many times, as he went along the way *meditating* on and singing of Jesus, he would forget his journey and invite all the elements to praise Jesus" (n. 115; Omn, 329). At first glance this tex seems to be merely repetitious and even childishly naive. A deeper study of it, however, reveals its power and striking beauty: this is Celano's dramatic way of showing what Francis' life was all about: that Francis was a man wholly caught up in Jesus. It was by having Christ in his heart and by "following" Christ in his mind, that Francis became spiritually one with his Lord.

Such "spiritual" following of Christ was also a key element in the prayer life of St. Clare. In order to become like Christ, Clare taught, a person must have him in one's heart and keep him ever before one's eyes. Such, indeed, is the thrust of the counsel which she gave to her spiritual daughter, Agnes of Prague.[32] *"Look upon* him," Clare writes, painting a vivid image of Jesus, "Who for thee became despised and follow him though thou become despised for his sake in this world. O noble queen, thy spouse, more beautiful than the sons of men, became for thy salvation the lowest of men, despised, struck, scourged untold times in his whole body, and died amidst the suffering of the cross." Having thus formed a portrait of the poor, suffering Jesus in the mind of Agnes, Clare then leads her to pray: ". . . *behold* him, *consider* him, *contemplate* him, and *desire* to imitate him!"

Clare herself became "conformed" to Christ not merely externally by living in very strict poverty but also interiorly by surrendering her heart to the Lord. By continually *meditating* on the sufferings of Christ and keeping his passion ever before her mind, she actually "co-suffered" with her Lord and even seemed "crucified with Jesus."[33] Such co-suffering with Christ and such deep meditation establishes a love-relationship with the Lord which perdures beyond death itself. "If thou suffer with him," Clare teaches Agnes, "thou shalt reign with him; if thou weep with him, thou shalt rejoice with him; if thou die with him on the cross of sorrow, thou shalt possess heavenly mansions in the brightness of the saints. . . "[34]

The above survey of the franciscan sources indicates that the following of Christ was a fundamental value for Francis and his brothers. Above all else the friars sought to love God and to surrender their hearts to him. They loved each other and all men who came into their lives. Furthermore, the brothers practiced and grew in the simplicity, humility and poverty to which the Gospel challenged them. Through word and example they preached the Good News of salvation and deepened their life of prayer. All this they did with the firm intention of following in the "footsteps" of Christ, for he was the very center of their way of life. Hence the words which St. Paul addressed to the Ephesians can also be applied to the friars: "You, too, are built upon the foundation laid by the apostles and prophets, the cornerstone being Christ himself. He is the one who holds the whole building together and makes it grow into a sacred temple in the Lord. In union with him you too are being built together with all the others into a house where God lives through his Spirit" (Eph 2:20–22).

* * * *

By emphasizing the following of Christ so dramatically, the primitive franciscan community revitalized the apostolic movements of their day. True, the image of the poor, suffering Christ was already the common heritage of the eleventh and twelfth centuries. With the notable exception of the itinerant preachers of France, however, this image of Christ for some reason failed to motivate the Christians of these centuries to model their lives directly on his. It was rather the example of the *apostles* and of the *early Church* which fired their imaginations and led them to reform Church institutions and to experiment with new forms of religious life.

The Gregorian Reform, for example, sought to revive the

ideals of the Christian life as described in the Acts of the Apostles. Even though he laid great stress on the historical life of Jesus, Peter Damian nonetheless referred to the *apostles* and the practices of the *early Church* in order to explain the ideal of both the monks and the Canons Regular.[35] Rupert of Deutz, too, taught that monastic life is modeled on the life of the apostles. According to Rupert, a life of humility and interior virtue, the hallmark of the Jerusalem community, constitutes the true monk and apostle.[36]

The itinerant preachers of France brought two fundamental changes to this trend. First of all they discarded this "inner" following of the apostles and of the early Church in favor of a very literal observance of the Gospels. That is, they imitated the life of the apostles by literally renouncing all possessions and going from place to place to preach the Kingdom of God. In this way they made the apostolic life the model of their day to day existence. Secondly, they expressly stressed the following of the poor, suffering Christ. Of Bernard of Thiron, for example, it was said: "Poor in spirit, he followed the poor Lord even to death."[37] Indeed, these itinerant preachers combined the following of the apostles and the following of Christ into a single, inseparable ideal. This is indicated in a statement referring to Vitalis of Savigny: ". . . he declared that the light yoke of Christ be carried by way of the apostles' footsteps."[38]

For some unexplainable reason, however, the various lay movements of the twelfth and early thirteenth centuries completely lost sight of the following of Christ and once again gave their full allegiance to the following of the apostles. Peter Waldo, for example, vowed to live in poverty and went about the city barefoot, preaching the Gospel. This he did with a determined, conscious desire to follow the example of the *apostles.* Because of their form of life, the later Waldenses considered themselves to be truly the *vicars of the apostles.* The Humiliati were most anxious to preach salvation to the people after the manner of the *apostles.* The Poor Catholics sought to live like the *apostles* and to imitate the *early Christians,* an ideal they closely shared with the community of Bernard Primus. This ideal, as Pope Gregory IX testifies, was also adopted by St. Dominic: "In him have I met a man who embodied the *life of the apostles* to its fullest extent!"[39]

With the coming of St. Francis and his followers, however, this "apostolic" element receded completely into the background and was replaced by a renewed emphasis on the following of *Christ.* Though many elements in the life of the Friars Minor closely resembled that of the earlier movements, their motivation and inspiration for living this kind of life were significantly different. Whereas the life of the *apostles* and the *example of the early Church* were the primary goals of most religious groups of these centuries, it was clearly the following of *Christ himself* which inspired the Friars Minor.

Obviously, there is no irreconcilable opposition between these two ideals, namely the following of *Christ* and the following of the *apostles.* In fact, the pre-franciscan movements, conscious of Paul's words, "Imitate me, just as I imitate Christ" (1 Cor 11:1), must have known that by imitating the apostles they were at the same time following in the footsteps of Christ. Nevertheless, it is significant that this latter term appears so infrequently in their sources.

On the other hand, the very use of terms in the franciscan sources clearly indicates that St. Francis and his followers did not consciously seek to imitate the apostles but rather to follow directly in the footsteps of Christ and to make him the very center of their lives. And they were not interested in restoring the *early* Church but rather in reforming their *contemporary* Church. Thomas of Celano calls Francis an "excellent craftsman," for "according to his plan, rule, and teaching, proclaimed before all, *the Church is being renewed* in both sexes, and the threefold army of those to be served is triumphing. To all he gave a norm of life, and he showed in truth the way of salvation in every walk of life" (1 Celano, 37; Omn, 260).

Out of sheer curiosity one is led to ask why such terms as *life of the apostles* and *life according to the form of the primitive Church* do not even appear in the writings of St. Francis and play only a very peripheral role in the other early franciscan sources. Very likely the answer lies in Francis' own religious experience. Because the Crucified Christ became such a central reality in his life, Francis was no longer concerned about imitating anyone else, not even the apostles, but only Christ.

To this one might well add a second reason, namely the troubled relationship which existed at that time between the Church and the apostolic movements. In this tense situation Francis planted himself firmly on the side of the Church and acted, though most often only indirectly, against the heretics. The influence which the presence of St. Francis had on both the heretics and the faithful is solemnly but truthfully described by Thomas of Celano: "The wickedness of heretics was confounded, the faith of the Church exalted; and while the faithful rejoiced, the heretics slipped secretly away. For such great signs of sanctity were evident in him that no one dared to oppose his words. . . . Francis thought that the faith of the holy Roman Church was by all means to be preserved, honored, and imitated, that faith in which alone is found the salvation of all who are to be saved. He revered priests and he had a great affection for every ecclesiastical order" (1 Celano, 62; Omn, 281). Because the two terms listed above became the common slogans and even war cries of contemporary heretical movements, Francis very likely avoided using them purposely in order to disassociate himself and his brothers completely from these rebelious movements.

Notes

1. See *Vita s. Francisci,* 9, 65 (AnalFranc X, 340, 365).

2. *Fourth Letter to Agnes,* 3 (Brady, p. 97).

3. *Commentary on the Rule,* ch. 3, 6, 12 (fol. 18r, 34v, 74v).

4. See *Non deberent* (BullFr. 23); *Nimis iniqua* (BullFr, 74, 75).

5. *Cronica* (Scalia, p. 63).

6. *Sermo 1. ad Fratres Minores,* ed. H. Felder (Rome, 1903), p.6.

7. *De perfectione evangelica,* q. 2, a. 2, concl. *(Opera omnia,* V, 142a).

8. See Dinkler-Schubert, "Christusbild," in RGG I, 1789-98; J. A. Jungmann, *Die Stellung Christi im liturgischen Gebt* (Munster, 1925), pp. 112-247.

9. See E. Kahler, "Nachfolge Christi (Dogmengeschichtlich)," in RGG IV, 1288-92.

10. Esser, "Die religiosen Bewegungen," p. 291.

11. See, for example, *Epistola 4* (PL 144, 314); *Sermo 18* (PL 144, 609); *De Dignitate sacerdotii* (Pl 145, 495).

12. *Expositio in regulam b. Augstini* (PL 176, 888).

13. *Vita s. Stephani* (PL 204, 1008).

14. Translated from the Latin found in M. von Dmitrewski, *Die christliche freiwillige Armut vom Ursprung der Kirche bis zum 12. Jahrhundert* (Berlin-Leipzig, 1913), p. 76. See also M. Bernards, "Nudus nudum Christum sequi," in WissWeish, 14 (1951), 148-51.

15. *Vita s. Bernardi* (PL 172, 1430).

16. See A Mitterrutzner, *Der hl. Franziskus van Assisi und die Armut. Eine genetische Darstellung seiner religiosen Anschauung von der Armut im Lichte der Quellen des 13. Jahrhunderts* (Brixen, 1961), p. 95.

17. *Admonition 1* (Omn, 77-78).

18. *Rule of 1221*, ch. 22 (Omn, 47).

19. *Letter to the Faithful* (Omn, 94).

20. *Rule of 1221*, ch. 22 (Omn, 49).

21. *Admonition 2* (Omn, 79).

22. *Rule of 1221*, ch. 22 (Omn, 94).

23. *Letter to the Faithful* (Omn, 94).

24. *Rule of 1223*, ch. 6 (Omn, 61-62).

25. *Historia Orientalis* (Omn, 1610).

26. *Rhetorica antiqua* (TestMin, 92).

27. *The Legend of St. Clare of Assisi*, 14 (Brady, p. 29).

28. *Cronica* (Scalia, p.63).

29. *Commentary on the Rule*, ch. 2, 4, 10 (fol. 124, 20v-21r, 58r-58v).

30. *Mirificans misericordias* (BullFr, 65).

31. For an analysis of Elias' encyclical see Lapsanski, pp. 61-65.

32. *Second Letter to Agnes*, 3 (Brady, p. 92).

33. *The Legend of St. Clare of Assisi*, 31 (Brady, p. 41).

34. *Second Letter to Agnes*, 3 (Brady, p. 92).

35. See *De communi vita canonicorum*, II (PL 145, 506).

36. See *De vita vere apostolica* (PL 170, 631 f.).

37. *Vita s. Bernardi* (PL 172, 1432).

38. Translated from the Latin found in Grundmann, p. 40, n. 57.

39. M. H. Vicaire, *Geschichte des hl. Dominikus* (Freiburg, 1962), II, 253 f.

4.

EVANGELICAL PERFECTION
IN THE LIFE
OF THE FRIARS MINOR

The themes examined in the previous two chapters of this study, namely, "Gospel Life" and the "Following of Christ," were no mere abstract ideals but rather dynamic values which the early community of brothers, inspired by their charismatic leader, adopted as their own and observed as their way of life. These same values, furthermore, directly and deeply influenced the way in which the brothers viewed themselves and their mission within the Church and the world at large.

1. Becoming a Friar Minor

How a person becomes a Friar Minor is nowhere so simply and yet so strikingly described as in the Testament of St. Francis. "When *God* gave me some friars," says Francis, as he recalls the early days of his new way of life. In these few words Francis indicates his belief that a vocation to religious life is precisely that, a *call,* an invitation given to the individual by the *Lord.* This same thought is repeated in the Form of Life which Francis gave to St. Clare: "Because it was *God* who *inspired* you to become daughters and hand-maids of the most high supreme King and Father of heaven and to espouse yourselves to the Holy Spirit . . ." (Omn, 76). Clearly, it is God who is the origin, the center and the goal of life in religion. He also provides the power that animates this way of life. Man need only to lay himself open to accept the Lord's call and to respond freely and lovingly to his working in his life.

This response took the form of "leaving the world": the friars turned away from their previous way of life and turned to the Lord. From now on they began to live differently and to be motivated by different values. "Those who embraced this life gave everything they had to the poor," writes Francis, summarizing the brothers' style of life. "They were *satisfied* with one habit which was patched inside and

outside, and a cord, and trousers. We *refused* to have anything more. Those of us who were clerics said the Office
like other clerics, while the lay brothers said the 'Our Father,' and we were *only too glad* to find shelter in abandoned
churches. We *made no claim* to learning and we were *sub-
missive* to everyone" (Testament; Omn, 68).

Such was the process of becoming a Friar Minor and the
way of life which Francis lived with his first companions.
Certainly the life was simple, even physically austere, for the
brothers had no possessions, wore poor clothing and had no
dwellings. Yet the thrust of the text seems to be not on
these external deprivations, but rather on the internal attitudes which filled the hearts of the brothers: they were *satisifed*
and *glad* to live so simply, they *refused* to have more; they
were satisfied *to be* and felt no compulsion to "get ahead."
These were men whose hearts were at peace. They knew
what they wanted and they were doing it, namely respond-
ing to God's call to them to live the Gospel.

By and large these elements which Francis lists as part of
the process of becoming a Friar Minor are preserved in the
later sources. Francis, Celano reports, using biblical imagery,
"ploughed up the land" by his preaching, "sowed the seed
of life," and brought forth "blessed fruit." Many persons,
coming into contact with him, "fled from the world" and
"followed Francis devoutly in his life and purpose through
the grace and the will of the Most High" (1 Celano, 56;
Omn, 275-76). Another text states that persons of all walks
of life, the rich and the poor, the lettered and the unlettered,
"led on by the spirit of God, came to put on the habit of
holy religion" (1 Celano, 31; Omn, 253-54).

According to these and other passages, an authentic "conversion" to the Order of Friars Minor revolves around three
elements, namely God, the world, and St. Francis. That is,
God inspires a person to turn away from the world—this

meant turning one's back on worldly values, selling one's goods and giving to the poor—and then to join himself to Francis by adopting his habit, teaching and way of life. This process of conversion was perfectly exemplified by Brother Bernard, the saint's first disciple. Bernard, writes Celano, *"hastened to sell all his goods* and *gave the money to the poor,* though not to his parents . . . When he had done this, he was associated with *St. Francis* by his life and by his habit, and he was always with him until, after the number of the brothers had increased, he was sent to other regions by obedience to his kind father. His *conversion to God* was a model to others in the manner of selling one's possessions and giving to the poor" (1 Celano, 24; Omn, 248–49).

The above model developed by Thomas of Celano to explain the process of becoming a Friar Minor is maintained with only minor variations by several other sources. Julian of Speyer expressed the friars' conversion in this way: ". . . after a short while certain men began to be animated by his [Francis'] example to penance and, having left all things, to be joined to him in habit and way of life."[1] Francis was an ideal guide, for he taught first by deeds and by the example of his own life and only later by words. The values he taught others, he first experienced in himself. Francis, himself instructed by "the grace of the Holy Spirit," encouraged his brother to cast their care "upon the Lord."[2]

The Legend of the Three Companions emphasizes that the spirit-filled life of Francis was like a magnet which attracted many to join him. "The power and truth of what he said did not come from any human source," the legend declares, indicating an important truth about Francis, "and his words impressed many learned and cultured men who hastened to see and hear him . . .Many of the people, nobles and commoners alike, were touched by *divine inspira-*

tion and began to imitate *Francis' way of life,* and to follow in his steps. They *abandoned the cares and pomps of
the world,* desiring to live under his direction, guidance,
and discipline" (n. 54; Omn, 937). Besides the usual elements of conversion, there is in this text a further development, namely the stress on "imitating Francis" and on
"following in the footsteps of Francis." Francis, whose
concern was "to follow in the footsteps of Christ," here
himself becomes the object of imitation. Francis' own life
thus becomes the model of franciscan life; his personal
charism becomes the property of the community.

Another passage in this legend describes entrance into the
Order by stating simply that some men came to Francis
and begged him to "receive them as brothers" (n. 35; Omn,
922). These few words are very meaningful, for they indicate
an essential characteristic of life in the Order, namely brotherhood. To become a Friar Minor meant to be accepted by
the brothers as a brother!

The liturgical texts report that men gave away all their
possessions, in this way became "lesser" in spirit and in
deed, and then joined themselves to Francis and followed
his direction.[3] Jordan of Giano telescopes the process of
becoming a Friar Minor by saying simply that a candidate
to the Order had "to sell all his possessions and give to the
poor."[4]

A few of the sources tend to speak of an "external"
and "internal" element in the conversion of the brothers.
This is clearly pinpointed in the following passage of 2
Celano: "The saint instructed those who came to the order
that first they should give a notice of dismissal to the world
by offering first their *outward possessions* to God and *then
themselves inwardly*" (n. 80; Omn, 429). What Francis here
demands of his followers is that they dispossess themselves
of all material goods and then surrender themselves completely to God.

In like manner St. Clare and her sisters surrendered their riches and inheritance and followed Christ. "At the beginning of her conversion," Celano writes about St. Clare, "she caused the paternal inheritance which had come to her to be sold and gave the proceeds to the poor, keeping nothing of the money for herself. Then *having left the world without,* though *enriched in mind within,* she *ran after Christ* unburdened by any possessions. So strict was the pact she thus entered with holy poverty and so great the love she had for it, that she would *have naught else but the Lord Jesus* nor wished her daughters to possess aught besides."[5] The papal documents add a somewhat ascetical and juridical aspect to the process of conversion: a person becomes a franciscan when he decides to leave the "emptiness" and "vain pleasures" of the world at the inspiration of God and begins to observe the form of life approved by the Church for the friars.[6]

2. The Biblical Self-Concept of the Friars Minor

The early sources have much to say about the process of becoming a Friar Minor, as well as about the life-style of St. Francis and his first brothers. These are important aspects of franciscan life and have relevance even for twentieth century franciscans. But perhaps even more important and more relevant is the exciting way in which the early sources made use of biblical concepts in order to explain the nature of the Order of Friars Minor. What these authors did was to study and meditate deeply on the data of revelation: on the themes, symbols and personages of the Bible. They then applied these biblical themes and symbols to the franciscan community, in order to clarify its nature and function.

In similar fashion, it will be recalled, the authors of the New Testament used symbols and categories of the Old

when speaking of Christ and the Christian community.[7]
It was by reflecting on such biblical themes as "mystery,"
"sheepfold," "Kingdom of God," "Holy City," "bride
of Christ," "People of God," etc., that the Fathers of the
Second Vatican Council, too, proclaimed the reality of the
Church to believers of the twentieth century.[8]

What is significant about this approach, whether one considers the Second Vatican Council or the early franciscan
sources, is the vivid consciousness in the minds of the
authors that Salvation History has not ceased with the writing of the final page of the New Testament, but that God
is dynamically present and active in each age of history.
In the thirteenth century, the franciscan sources proclaim,
God raised up St. Francis and his Order to carry out his
work. In the twentieth, the Fathers of Vatican II declare,
God is continuing to use the Church of Christ to reveal
his love to mankind!

A simple yet meaningful example of this approach is
found in the biography of Francis by Julian of Speyer. A
number of times Julian applies the scriptural phrase "little
Flock" (Lk 12:32) to Francis and his first followers.[9] By
using this term Julian emphasizes the brothers' simplicity,
helplessness, and lack of numbers, but also their total reliance on God. Francis' stress on dependence on God, the
essential characteristic of his view of poverty, reveals that
Francis, consciously or unconsciously, considered his brotherhood to be the *anawim,* the "Poor of the Lord."[10]

Thomas of Celano uses the biblical symbols of "vine"
and "vineyard of the Lord" (Jer 2:21) in reference to the
Friars Minor. The Order founded by Francis, Celano maintains, is a "new *chosen vineyard* that the hand of the Lord
has so kindly planted in the world" (1 Celano, 74; Omn,
290-91). Through St. Francis, the same author writes, a new
Order "was *planted* in the desert of this world . . . a *fruitful*

vine bearing flowers of sweetness unto the odor of holy vir-
tues by extending everywhere the *branches* of a sacred religion" (n. 89; Omn, 302). The Order, states 2 Celano, is
"the vineyard of the Lord" (n. 24; Omn, 382).

Even more dramatic is the theological meditation dis-
cernible in the Encyclical Letter of Brother Elias.[11] In this
writing Elias makes extensive and profound use of the biblical
category "People of God" in order to explain the nature of
the franciscan community. The friars, Elias proclaims with
conviction, really constitute a "new nation" within the framework of Salvation History. They are a "new Israel," because
Francis, the "new Moses," gave to them a "rule of life"
and a "testament of peace." What is more, the friars also
bear an intimate relationship to the community of the New
Testament. Because St. Francis preached the "Kingdom
of God" to his brothers, just like Christ did to his hearers,
the friars are indeed a "new People of God" (cf. Lk 1:17).[12]

A very similar image of the Order of Friars Minor is
found in the pages of the *Sacrum Commercium.* Here the
author emphasizes that Christ established the New Covenant
by shedding his blood on the cross. But the cross and the
shedding of blood, the author maintains, were nothing else
than Christ's perfect and complete "emptying" of himself:
the summation and the highest expression of his life-long
poverty. This connection between poverty and the cross of
Christ is vividly pictured in the following passage of the
work: "You [Lady Poverty] were with him [Christ] when
the Jews reviled him, when the pharisees insulted him, when
the chief priests cursed him; you were with him when he
was buffeted, spit upon, and scouraged, He who should have
been respected by all was mocked by all, and you alone com-
forted him. You did not leave him unto death, 'even to death
on a cross.' And on the cross itself, *when he hung there
naked,* his arms outstretched, his hands and feet pierced,

you suffered with him, so that nothing in him should appear more glorious than you" (n. 21; Omn, 1563).

Because of this intimate connection between poverty and the cross of Christ, the friars, by being faithful to their own voluntary poverty, can enter into Christ's "new covenant" and become the "new people of God." Indeed, poverty is the "seal of the kingdom of heaven" with which the "elect" are sealed; it is for this seal of election that the friars yearn (n. 21, 22). The friars are "unencumbered" and have cast away "all their burdens"; they are thus externally and internally poor. Since they are so free and open of heart, they are invited to enter into a "covenant of peace" with Lady Poverty, and with the Lord, and thereby to become "servants" and the "sheep of his flock."[13] Truly, the Friars Minor are "the seed which the Lord has blessed (Is 61:9) and has chosen in unaffected love" (2 Cor 6:6).[14] As is apparent, what we are dealing with here is an interpretation of the Franciscan Order by way of biblical symbols.

Pope Gregory IX, too, makes use of the words of Scripture in order to say something meaningful about the Friars Minor. The friars foil the enemies of the Church, maintains the Pope, because they wear the "breastplate of justice" and the "helmet of salvation." In one hand they carry the "shield of faith" to ward off the fiery arrows of the enemy, while in the other they wield the "sword of the Spirit," which is the Word of God (Eph 6:14, 16, 17). These brothers, by preaching God's Word and by living in voluntary poverty, are authentic "men of the Gospel," says the Pope.[15]

The sources examined above lead one to assert that the Friars Minor viewed themselves as a new power which burst upon the world. In the words of the liturgical texts, they were a "new Order" and a "new way of life," a vast army which St. Francis led into battle against the forces of evil.[16] This spiritual army, one can well add, appropriated to itself the identity and incarnated in its own way of life the values which St. Paul listed in his letter to the Colossians: "You are the *people of God;* he loved you and chose you for his own. So then, you must put on *compassion, kindness, humility, gentleness,* and *patience* . . . You must *forgive* each other in the same way that the Lord has forgiven you. And to all these add *love,* which binds all things together in perfect unity. The *peace* that Christ gives is to be the judge in your hearts; for to this peace God has called you together in the one body. And be *thankful.* Christ's message, in all its richness, must live in your hearts" (Col 3:12-16). This message of Christ took root in the heart of Francis and his brothers. It is this message and these values which transformed their lives and indicated to them what their brotherhood was all about.

3. The Gospel Life and the Friars' Mission in Salvation History

The early sources, which formulated the biblical self-concept of the franciscan community so dramatically, also speak with great enthusiasm of the spiritual mission which this "new people" exercises at God's bidding within the present economy of salvation. In a beautiful passage of his Letter to the Chapter (Omn, 104), Francis encourages his brothers to hear the "voice of the Son of God," to keep his commandments "wholeheartedly" and to practice his "counsels" with all their mind. He tells them, using the words of Scripture, to "give thanks to the Lord, for he is good" (Ps 135:1) and to "extol him" in their works (Tb 13:6). Finally he explains to them their mission in these powerful words: "this is the very reason he has sent you all over the world, so that by word and deed you might *bear witness* to his message and *convince everyone that there is*

no other almighty God besides him" (Tb 13:4). The friars'
basic apostolate, as expressed in these words, is nothing else
than to love God, to praise him, and to bear witness to
others through one's own life that God is great!

This is the same message which Francis shares with his
brothers so ecstatically in the Rule of 1221. He writes:
"With all our hearts and all our souls, all our minds and
all our strength, all our power and all our understanding,
with every faculty and every effort, with every affection and
all our emotions, with every wish and desire, we should love
our Lord and God . . . Nothing, then, must keep us back,
nothing separate us from him, nothing come between us and
him. At all times and seasons, in every country and place,
every day and all day, we must have a true and humble
faith, and keep him in our hearts, where we must love,
honour, adore, serve, praise and bless, glorify and acclaim,
magnify and thank, the most high supreme and eternal God
. . ." (ch. 23; Omn, 52). These are the words of a man who
is drunk on God, a man who is spending his entire life in
loving God and praising him. This same man in these same
words is telling his brothers to do just that, for there is no
better and happier life imaginable.

Indeed, it is no exaggeration to say that Francis wanted
his brothers to form a kind of eschatological community
gathered about the throne of God for the purpose of praising him. It must have been with this view in mind that Francis put together a series of praises from the Scriptures and
which he wanted his brothers to recite antiphonally. Here
are some verses from that compilation: "Holy, holy, holy,
the Lord God almighty, who was, and who is, and who is
coming . . ." (Rv 4:8). "Worthy are thou, O Lord our
God, to receive glory and honour and power . . . " (Rv
4:11). "Bless the Lord, all you works of the Lord" (Dn
3:57). And the response after each verse is this: "Let us

praise and glorify him forever" (Omn, 138).

Another aspect of the spiritual mission entrusted to the friars consists in being faithful to the way of life which the Lord revealed to Francis. They are to be what their very name implies, namely "Friars Minor," lesser brothers! They were indeed "lowly," "subject to all" and "founded solidly in true humility," declares Thomas of Celano. And they were *brothers* because their hearts were filled with love for one another. "O with what ardor of *charity* the new disciples of Christ burned!" reports Celano enthusiastically. "How great was the *love* that flourished in the members of the members of this pious society! For whenever they came together anywhere, or met one another along the way, as the custom is, there a shoot of *spiritual love* sprang up, sprinkling over all *love* the seed of *true affection*" (1 Celano, 38; Omn, 260-61).

The friars' mission of being *lesser brothers* one to another overflowed to the larger community. It is precisely by being *minors,* Celano maintained, that the friars fulfill a very important mission within the Church of Christ. By their humble and simple style of life, and by their readiness to always take the last place, they indicate to the faithful what it means to follow Christ and to be faithful to the ideals of the primitive Church. This is certainly the thrust of the words which Celano has Francis say to Hugolin, when the cardinal expressed to him a plan for reforming the Church which included consecrating the friars as bishops. Francis said to him: "Lord, my brothers are called *minors* so that they will not presume to become greater. Their vocation teaches them to remain in a *lowly station* and to follow in the footsteps of the *humble* Christ . . . . If you want them to bear fruit for the church of God, hold them and preserve them in the station to which they have been called, and bring them back to a *lowly station,* even if they are unwilling" (2 Celano, 148; Omn, 481-82). Not by becoming prelates and mighty will the friars best serve the Church, but by remaining *lesser brothers*, Francis maintained.

It is by being faithful to the values of brotherhood and minority that the friars fulfill the "mystery of the Gospel." They serve as "beacons of light" which "in these latest times" lead mankind away from the sinful world to the love of Jesus Christ (2 Celano, 155, 157; Omn, 486, 488). In his *Treatise on the Miracles*, Celano broaches a similar theme. By incarnating the "perfection of the early Church" in their lives, he declares, Francis, the "new man," and his "new army" are transforming and renewing the "old world" which was corrupted by sin.[17]

The above reflections indicate clearly that the mission of the friars is not limited to personal sanctification, but is significantly "other" directed. Francis chose not "to live for himself alone," for he was deeply conscious that the Lord sent him to "win souls for God" (1 Celano, 35; Omn, 258). The *Legend of the Three Companions* emphasizes this same theme. By living the Gospel and by exhorting others to adopt the same values, the friars would bring many persons to the Lord. "Dear Brothers," Francis is quoted as saying to his companions, "let us consider our vocation, and how God, in his great mercy, called us *not only for our salvation but for that of many;* and to this end we are to go through the world exhorting all men and women by our example as well as by our words to do penance for their sins, and to live keeping in mind the commandments of God." Then Francis encouraged his *lesser brothers* with these words: "Do not be afraid to preach penance even though we appear ignorant and of no account. *Put your trust in God* who overcame the world; hope steadfastly in him who, by the Holy Spirit, *speaks through you* to exhort all to be converted to him and to observe his commandments" (n. 36; Omn, 924).

These words certainly reveal the heart of Francis, but they also indicate his view of the nature and mission of the Order he founded.

Pope Gregory IX expressed a similar thought when he declared that the friars are "new vinedressors" whom the Lord sent at this "eleventh" hour to bring about the salvation of the world.[18] To this, Burkhard of Ursperg added that by their way of life, especially by their voluntary simplicity and poverty, the friars are renewing the Church and at the same time offsetting the evil influence of heretical "apostolic" groups.[19] Finally, by their love, lowliness and penance the friars are slowly restoring in themselves the very blessedness of paradise, which the first man lost by his sin.

A few of the sources go so far as to invest the friars with an almost apocalyptic mission. They are like the "defenders of the ramparts of Jerusalem," maintained Jacques de Vitry, for they protect the inhabitants of the world from evil. These poor and simple friars are the "bodyguards of Solomon" and the "light of the world" sent by God in these "last days" in order to confound Antichrist and his henchmen.[20] This the friars accomplished, it should be pointed out, by combating the heresies which afflicted the Church of their day.

Finally, Salimbene, under Joachimist influence, identified the Friars Minor, these men of simplicity, humility and prayer, with one of the Orders which was to initiate the age of the Holy Spirit. This view can, of course, be set aside. But he did express the beautiful thought that the friars, like the prophets of old, are to heal the spiritual wounds of mankind![21]

* * * *

This pervasive consciousness that the Friars Minor constitute a " new nation," a new "Israel," and that God entrusted them with an important spiritual mission to the Church and the world distinguishes the early franciscans from previous apostolic movements. The self-concept of these earlier groups was, one is led to say, much less imaginative and much more humble. Previous movements modeled their lives and apostolate on ancient structures, like the example of the apostles and the early Church; they considered themselves to be the "poor of Christ," a term expressly used by such varied figures as Hugh of St. Victor, Stephan of Thiers-Muret, Robert of Arbrissel, Bernard of Thiron, and the Waldenses. The Friars Minor, however, went far beyond this imagery. They burst upon the world with the dramatic conviction and exciting vision that they were God's special instruments within the on-going history of salvation.

At first glance it may seem incongrous, even shocking, that these poor and unlearned men of Assisi should have such a noble, not to say arrogant, view of themselves and their mission. Yet this conviction and self-confidence seems to be a logical consequence of their profound dedication to the Gospel. After all, the Friars Minor—true to the example of Christ—trod the path of self-emptying. They "emptied" their hearts of all earthly possessions, attachments, concerns and selfishness. By so doing, they made plenty of room for God in their hearts and made it possible for him to take over their lives. And this is preciesely what the Lord did, as so many of the sources indicate. In a word, because the friars surrendered themselves so perfectly to the Divine Will, the Lord was able to use them as pliable instruments for carrying out his work. Of this the friars were very conscious.

It is therefore important to note that the self-confidence which St. Francis and his brothers had in their community and in their mission is not at all based on a high opinion of self, that is, on their personal holiness or merit, but rather on the vivid experience of God's loving-kindness and on the deep conviction that the Lord has filled them and is using them as his instruments for bringing about his own ends, namely, the salvation of many persons. Such a deep-seated conviction is not noticeable among the previous apostolic groups.

The friars were conscious that God's power in man is strongest and most effective when man is weak and admits his dependence on the Lord (2 Cor 12:9). By being *minores* they adopted the attitude of heart and received the consequent promise which are described by the Psalmist when he says:

> Trust in the Lord and do good;
> live in the land and be safe.
> Seek your happiness with the Lord,
> and he will give you what you most want.

> Give yourself to the Lord;
> trust in him, and he will help you;
> he will cause your goodness to shine as the light
> and your righteousness as the noonday sun
> (Ps 37:3-6).

* * * *

It must be pointed out, however, that the above-summarized conviction of the friars in regard to their mission was no mere theoretical matter. On the concrete level the friars performed a multi-faceted service for and within the Church. Salimbene reports that the friars undertook works of corporal mercy, e.g. they buried persons killed in a massacre. One of the friars was an inquisitor of the faith for a certain time. Their main service, however, consisted in ministry: in preaching, hearing confessions and giving counsel.[22]

Whenever and wherever there was a need in the Church, point out the papal documents, the friars made themselves available for service. Some, for example, preached the Crusade to free the Holy Places; others were sent on missionary ventures to convert the Tartars; many brought the word of God to Saracens and other non-believers.[23] All these apostolic missions, it must be noted, were the logical consequence of the friars' fidelity to their Gospel life, particularly to Christ's missionary discourse. The popes recognized that the friars' way of life made them effective legates and missionaries, especially in their confrontations with heretics. Pope Innocent IV declared that the friars were "more useful" to the Church than others because they follow "the humility of our Savior."[24]

Notes

1. *Vita s. Francisci,* 17 (AnalFranc X, 342).

2. Ibid., 19, 24 (AnalFranc X, 343, 346).

3. See *Legenda choralis Carnotensis,* 6 (AnalFranc X, 539); *Legenda Vaticana,* 8 (AnalFranc X, 532).

4. *Chronicle,* 1,2,9 (Hermann, pp. 20, 21, 25).

5. *The Legend of St. Clare of Assisi,* 13 (Brady, p. 28).

6. *Cum dilecti filii* (BullFr, 2).

7. See C.K. Barrett, "The Bible in the New Testament Period," in D. E. Nineham (ed.), *The Church's Use of the Bible: Past and Present* (London, 1963), pp. 1-24.

8. See "Dogmatic Constitution on the Church," in Walter M. Abbot (ed.), *The Documents of Vatican II* (Geoffrey Chapman), pp. 14-96.

9. *Vita s. Francisci,* 17, 20 (AnalFranc X, 343, 344).

10. See 2 Celano, 70 (Omn, 423); van Corstanje, pp. 98-103.

11. See the analysis of this text in Lapsanski, pp. 65-66.

12. *Encyclical Letter,* 2,3 (van Corstanje, pp. 125, 126).

13. *Sacrum Commercium,* 14, 57 (Omn, 1559, 1589-90). See also the analysis of this source in Lapsanski, pp. 76-80.

14. *Sacrum Commercium,* 14 (Omn, p. 1559).

15. See *Licet Sacrosancta* (BullFr, 34); *Cum dilectos filios* (BullFr, 35).

16. *Sanctitatis nova signa,* 3 (AnalFranc X, 402); *Caput draconis,* 6 (AnalFranc X, 401).

17. 3 Celano, 1 (AnalFranc X, 271).

18. See *Cum messis multa* (BullFr, 100 f.).

19. *Chronicon* (TestMin, 17 f.).

20. *Historia Orientalis* (Omn, 1610, 1613).

21. *Cronica* (Scalia, pp. 28 f., 419, 422, 639, 933).

22. *Cronica* (Scalia, pp. 286, 633).

23. See *Pium, et sanctum* (BullFr, 139); *Vocem in excelso* (BullFr, 296); *Cum non solum homines* (BullFr, 353); *Pro zelo Fidei Christiane* (BullFr, 103); *Cum hora undecima* (BullFr, 360).

24. *Cum simus super Apostolicae* (BullFr, 359).

5.

EVANGELICAL PERFECTION
AND
POVERTY

Once St. Francis donned the simple cloak of a hermit; threw away his staff and kicked off his sandals in a joyful and literal response to Christ's words to his apostles (Mt 10:7-13),[1] poverty became an essential element of his Gospel way of life. That this was to be not merely his personal response but also that of his followers became clear when he opened the Gospel book three times to learn how he and his brothers were to live. At the first opening Francis and his two companions, Bernard and Peter, learned that if they wished to be perfect, they must go and sell all their goods and give to the poor (Mt 19:21). The second text directed them not to own two tunics, nor to take any provisions with them on their journeys (Lk 9:3), while the third taught them the importance of self-abnegation and the carrying of one's cross (Lk 9:23; Mt 16:24).

The response of Francis and his companions to these challenges of the Gospel is accurately reported in this passage of the *Legend of the Three Companions:* "Each time he opened the book blessed Francis *gave thanks to God* for this threefold confirmation and the resolution and desire which he had long held in his heart; and he said to the aforementioned Bernard and Peter: 'O Brothers, this is *our life and rule* and the life and rule of all those who may wish to join us. Go, therefore, and act on what you have heard.'"[2] The brothers did precisely that: they acted on what they had heard. As a result, poverty thereafter came to be closely associated with the friars' "life according to the form of the holy Gospel."

The early franciscan sources also emphasized the image of the *poor* Christ. That Christ was born in a lowly stable, that he was even buried in a sepulchre belonging to someone else, were events which were graphically etched in the minds of these franciscan authors.[3] St. Francis, too, had this same image of Christ in his mind. And he often shared this image with his brothers, as Thomas of Celano reports: "*Often*, indeed, speaking of poverty, he [Francis] would propose to his brothers this saying of the Gospel: 'the foxes have dens and the birds of the air have nests; but the Son of Man has nowhere to lay his head' " (Mt 8:20; Lk 9:58).[4] Because the image of the poor Christ made such a deep impression on the early friars, it is not surprising that they came to associate the concept of "following in the footsteps of Christ" with living in poverty.

This intimate relationship which poverty enjoyed with the friars' Gospel life and with their following of Christ was pointed out in previous chapters of this study. But because of the important and unique role which poverty has played within the Franciscan Order, it certainly merits a separate study.

1. Poverty as a Multi-faceted Value

By way of introduction it should be noted that the franciscan sources do not present a single, unified concept of poverty. Rather, poverty appears as a dynamic reality undergoing changes of growth and diminution with the passing of years. At times the concept of poverty is very rich and is bound up with other important values of Christian living. At other times the concept is very specific and lean. This difference makes it possible for one to speak of two quite distinct "views" of poverty, or even of two "trends" of development.

Some of the sources, for example, viewed poverty as a "fundamental attitude pervading the entire man," whereby external poverty was "merely the expression of a deeper, inward destitution with far vaster implications."[5] Other sources lost sight of this inner, spiritual dimension of poverty and concentrated on its external, ascetical aspects. In some-what broad strokes the following study intends to investigate the evolution which the concept of poverty underwent in the early franciscan sources.[6]

a. Poverty as a Basic Attitude of the Entire Person[7]

In the writings of St. Francis, life "without possessions" is a many-faced concept which embraces man's relationship not only to material goods, but also to his fellowmen and even to God. The saint wanted his brothers to live in mater-ial poverty, that is, to "empty" their hearts of all attach-ment to earthly goods. Upon entering the Order, for example, the friars were to sell all their possessions. Henceforth they were to wear only rough clothing and simple sandals instead of shoes. They were not to own anything whatever, not even houses, and were not to receive money.[8]

Francis also wanted his followers to "empty" their hearts of all immaterial goods as well, that is, of all values of which a man can be innerly proud. One such immaterial "posses-sion" against which Francis particularly warned his followers was selfish ambition which urges a person to be held in es-teem and to be in control of others. To those who hold office within the brotherhood, Francis addressed these poig-nant words: "The ministers and preachers must remember that *they do not have a right* to the office of serving the friars or of preaching, and so they must be prepared *to lay it aside* without objection the moment they are told to do so" (Rule of 1221, ch.17; Omn, 44). If they "claim" an office as their own and treat it as a personal "pos-session," they violate poverty and "incur risk to their souls" (Admonition 4; Omn, 80).

Francis also encouraged his brothers to "let go" of other

inner possessions such as anxieties of heart, envy, anger, concern for others' opinion, etc. According to Francis, a person is poor only to the extent to which he has "emptied" himself of selfishness and has "died" to his old self. Such a person can cope with various situations in life without becoming innerly disturbed. He can even "turn the other cheek," for he is a man of peace and considers himself the servant of all.[9] In these demands Francis is certainly not encouraging his brothers to develop a negative self-concept. Far from it. Rather, it is only the mature and integrated person, a person who is innerly secure, who can undergo the process of "letting go" which Francis described.

Finally, Francis wanted his brothers to "empty" their hearts of all *spiritual* security as well. He wanted his brothers to stand before God with outstretched arms, in complete nakedness of spirit, shorn of all claims to personal merit or virtue and acknowledging that whatever good they have or do is to be credited to God alone. "We must refer every good to the most high supreme God," writes Francis, "acknowledging that *all good belongs to him;* and we must thank him for it all, because *all good comes from him.*"[10] A man need only lay himself open, need only to "empty" himself of self, so that the Lord may use him as an instrument or channel to accomplish his will.

In a word, poverty, as conceived and lived by the simple man of Assisi, "implies the renuncation of all the goods of this world—i.e., of everything which might in any way at all furnish security and protection for human life. As a stranger and pilgrim, the truly poor man goes through life without a dwelling, without rights or protection, without goods or security even before God."[11] A man in whom this process of "letting go" has taken firm root can say with Francis, "My God and my all!" Such a man can also address to the Lord these words of the Psalmist:

I am always with you,
    and you hold me by the hand.
You guide me with your advice,
    and at the end you will receive me
with honor.
    What else do I have in heaven but you?
since I have you, what else do I want
    on earth?
My mind and my body may grow weak,
    but God is my strength;
he is all I ever want!

. . . as for me, how wonderful to be near God!
In the Lord God I find protection,
    to proclaim all that he has done (Ps 73:
    23-28).

·The motive which impelled St. Francis to take up this way of life was the example of Christ, the God-Man who emptied himself of his eternal riches in the mystery of the Incarnation[12] and who continues to humble himself daily in the mystery of the Eucharist.[13] Francis' view of poverty can therefore be called the "mystery of poverty," for it is based on and helps to clarify the mystery of Christ, the incarnate Son of God.[14]

A similar stress on the practice of external poverty, grounded on the example of Christ, and combined with a deeply spiritual vision characterizes the view which several other sources have concerning poverty. In 1 Celano, for example, poverty means separating oneself from the things of this world in order to become free for the Kingdom of God. By "emptying" himself of all self-will and temporal attachments, a man creates room in his heart and gives God a chance to enter.

Poverty understood in this way is closely allied to and is indeed a necessary prerequisite for a deep life of prayer. Francis' "greatest concern," reports Celano, "was *to be free from everything of this world,* lest the serenity of his mind be disturbed even for an hour by the taint of anything that was mere dust. He made himself insensible to all external noise, and . . . *occupied himself with God alone.* . . . With fruitful devotion he frequented only heavenly dwellings, and he who had *totally emptied himself* remained so much the longer in the wounds of the Savior" (n. 71; Omn, 288). Only the person who has "let go" of inner possessions can pray deeply, for prayer, too, is a "letting go," a surrender of the self to the Lord.

This inner attitude of heart, of course, must be expressed externally, as exemplified in Francis' own life of strict poverty and in his demand that his followers live without any superfluities. "With all zeal, with all solicitude," writes Celano, "he [Francis] guarded holy Lady Poverty, not permitting any vessel of any kind to be in the house, lest it lead to superfluous things, when he could in some way avoid being subject to extreme necessity without it. For, he used to say, it is impossible to satisfy necessity and not give in to pleasure" (n. 51; Omn, 272), This text, of course, does refflect the *author's intention* of presenting Francis as the model of asceticism. In regard to this passage, as also in regard to many other passages in the early franciscan sources, one must pose this question: to what extent are we confronted here with the historical Francis, and to what extent with the traditional "model" of a saint and ascetic which the author garnered from previous literature?[15]

In similar fashion 2 Celano emphasizes Francis' zeal for poverty. Francis "hated" money, Celano points out over and over again;[16] he was satisfied with the simplest clothing, namely a single tunic, cord and drawers. Because Francis was able to "let go" of possessions and to live so simply, he was truly a free man, inwardly and outwardly. Celano points this out in striking fashion when he writes: Francis "went his way *happy, secure,* and *confident;* he rejoiced to exchange a perishable treasure for the hundredfold" (n. 55; Omn, 411). Indeed, Francis and his brothers became the "poorest of the poor" *for the sake of Christ.* This kind of poverty brings joy and fulfillment, as Francis explains to his companion: "Do you think that evangelical poverty has nothing about it to be envied? *It has Christ* and through him it has all things in all" (n. 84; Omn, 432).

Poverty is a "royal" virtue, for it "shone forth so eminently" in Jesus and Mary, the King and Queen. Poverty was the road which led him to the Father. In this sense to "follow" Christ means to live in evangelical poverty. For the brothers, Christ's "way" became their "way" to the heavenly Father. It is through poverty, more than through any other virtue, that one becomes "a close friend of Christ," truly "Christ-like." For this reason does Francis call poverty "the special way of salvation (n. 200; Omn, 522). And the brothers by freely choosing poverty as their own way of life out of love for Christ are becoming "heirs and kings of the kingdom of heaven" (Rule of 1223, ch. 6; Omn, 61).

This view of poverty is evident also in the spirituality of St. Clare. Though she lay even greater stress on external poverty than did Francis, her motive for living in poverty remained the same as his, namely, the following of Christ. She wished to be perfectly poor because "the Lord made Himself poor for us in this world."[17]

Julian of Speyer, it must be added, echoes a similar theme. By divesting himself of all earthly possessions, Francis attained a high degree of conformity with the poor, crucified Christ, writes Julian.[18] By putting aside all cares and anxieties of heart, he became totally free for the service of God.

The same was true of the first friars.[19] The pact which they
made with poverty freed their hearts from greed and cares,
so that they enjoyed great inner harmony, peace and joy.
They spent much time in praising the Lord and in thanking
him for his mercy.[20]

These very positive consequences of living in poverty appear
also in the *Legend of the Three Companions.* Francis, the
legend points out, became totally poor out of love for the
poor Christ. Thus "freed" from all possessions, cares and
anxieties, he became truly "free" of heart, so that he went
about the city streets joyfully praising the Lord like one ine-
ebriated with the Spirit (n. 21; Omn, 911). This voluntary
"letting go" of all things for the Lord also made the brothers innerly free and joyful. "The brothers were able to
rejoice so truly in poverty," the legend reports, "because
they did not desire riches and despised all passing things
such as are pursued by those who love this world. . . .
They *rejoiced continually in the Lord* because, in themselves,
and between each other, there existed nothing to disturb
them. The more they were separated from the world, the
closer became their *union with God*" (n. 45; Omn, 931).
Poverty was for the brothers a means of becoming ever more
open to each other and to the Lord.

The most complete and the deepest view of franciscan poverty, however, is presented in the *Sacrum Commercium.* On
the one hand this "mystery play" faithfully transmits many
of the themes summarized above. It proclaims that to become
truly "poor" a man must disrobe himself of all earthly burdens, free himself from sin, and surrender his heart and will
to the Lord.

When Francis asked the elderly men, one representing the
Old Testament and the other the New, how he might come
to find the Lady Poverty, they gave him this answer: ". . .
if you want to get to her, remove the garments of your re-

joicing, and put away every encumbrance of sin entangling you, for unless you are stripped of these things, you cannot go up to her who dwells so high above" (n. 11; Omn, 1556). In this context poverty is the process of putting off the "old" man and putting on the "new." The poor man is one who freely chooses not to possess anything, so that he might be free to possess God and be filled with his Spirit. Such perfect poverty allows a man to taste how sweet God is and gives him a foretaste of heaven already in this life.[21]

On the other hand, the *Sacrum Commercium* dramatically broadens the horizon wherein poverty is operative by presenting it as God's principle of salvation. Poverty, to whom the Lord gave "the keys of the kingdom of heaven,"[22] is God's way of leading mankind to salvation not only during the Old and New Testaments, but likewise during the entire course of Church history.[23] Indeed, poverty is a sign that one belongs to the elect of the Lord. "You need have no doubt, no hesitance, about the possession of the kingdom of heaven," Lady Poverty tells the friars when she reflects on their fidelity to her, "for you *already possess* an *earnest of your future inheritance* and you have already *received* the *pledge* of the Holy Spirit, for you are stamped with the *seal* of the glory of Christ" (n. 65; Omn, 1594). This seal is their life of poverty.

God's mysterious and unaccountable ways are also the point of departure for the interpretation of poverty found in Celano's *Treatise on the Miracles*. Because of its dire poverty, the Order of. Friars Minor had no chance of survival from a human standpoint. But God, who intervened in Abraham's hopeless situation by granting him a son, also intervened in behalf of the sterile Order. By transforming its poverty into a principle of fecundity, he brought about a miraculous growth of the Order. "Not well-filled cellars and bulging larders, not extensive possessions govern this Order," writes Thomas of Celano, "but rather the same poverty which makes it worthy of heaven, nourishes it wondrously also on the earth."[24] What is here emphasized is the connection between poverty and providence. The poverty of the friars leads them to rely wholly on the Lord's providence for their sustenance. And he in his goodness does bless them and sustain them spiritually, and even physically!

The poverty expounded in the *Sacrum Commercium* and in the *Treatise on the Miracles,* it will be noticed, is no longer the fluid and unreflected mosaic that one finds in 1 and 2 Celano, the *Legend of the Three Companions,* the Chronicles and other early sources, but rather a well thought-out principle of franciscan life. Later thinkers, such as St. Bonaventure, continued this incipient trend by systematizing the franciscan view of poverty and by buttressing their teaching with theological reasoning and argumentation. St. Bonaventure, for example, did this in his work, *Quaestio de paupertate,* wherein he sought to formulate the "foundations of franciscan poverty from a scientific standpoint,"[25] against William of St. Armour, a professor in Paris. In this writing Bonaventure declared as follows: " . . . to renounce everything, both privately and in common, belongs to Christian perfection. . . . it is the principal counsel of evangelical perfection, as well as its fundamental principle and sublime foundation."[26]

Poverty is first of all the "principal counsel" of evangelical perfection, for it leads it followers to other counsels. The one who retains nothing for himself can more easily mortify his flesh and perfectly abnegate his own will. Bonaventure goes on to emphasize that the "foundation" of perfection is charity. But this charity, he maintains, is most perfect only when it excludes avarice, for this vice is the arch-enemy of charity. But a person who dispossess himself of all things in fact and in spirit effectively expels avarice from his heart. For this reason poverty is the "fundamental principle" of evangelical perfection. Bonaventure writes: "As the root of all evil is avarice, so is the highest poverty the root and principle of perfection."[27]

Finally, poverty is the "sublime foundation" of evangelical perfection. This is so, maintains Bonaventure, because it enables a man to lead the higher form of life, namely that of contemplation. Indeed, the man most capable of contemplation is the one who is completely stripped of temporal burdens: "whose kingdom is not of this world." Such a poor man has already laid the foundations of his heavenly dwelling. Such, indeed, is the kind of poverty practiced by the Friars Minor.[28]

* * * *

In their life of poverty, the Friars Minor certainly made their own the attitudes of heart which St. Paul describes when he says of himself: " . . . I have learned to be satisfied with what I have. I know what it is to be in need, and what it is to have more than enough. I have learned this secret, so that anywhere, at any time, I am content, whether I am full or hungry, whether I have too much or too little. I have strength to face all conditions by the power that Christ gives me" (Phil 4:11-13). In their poverty, the friars, too, learned the secret of how to be content in all situations, because they lived for Christ and received their power from him.

The franciscan view of poverty summarized above also reflects several important themes developed in the course of the centuries. In the early Church possessions were considered from the viewpoint of stewardship, that is, as goods to be shared with the poor and the less fortunate. Grounding themselves in the New Testament teaching, early writers like Origen, Cyprian, Marcion and Hermas stressed the value of poverty of spirit for Christians. Continuing this same line of thought, Clement of Alexandria considered poverty of spirit a great support of love of God and neighbor. To this poverty was soon added the practice of material poverty. Before entering the desert, for example, the hermits gave away all their possessions.[29]

As a way of day-to-day living, however, franciscan poverty was more immediately grounded in the apostolic movements of the eleventh and twelfth centuries. Already Stephan of Thiers-Muret practiced a modified form of communal poverty, an ideal which was later juridically approved and practiced not only by the Poor Catholics and the community of Bernard Primus, but by the mendicant orders as well. Stephan's view that poverty embraces not only things but the very self of a person[30] was later repeated by St. Francis. Moreover, Stephan's teaching that poverty opens up to its followers the road to salvation closely resembles Celano's description of poverty as "the special way of salvation." The thought underlying both views is that Christ made his way to heaven by way of poverty.

The itinerant preachers of France, bearded, unshod, wearing rough clothing, and having no place to lay their head, were particularly vivid precursors of the friars' poverty. Such poverty led both the itinerant preachers and the Friars Minor to open themselves completely to the Lord and to develop a deep trust in his loving mercy. As Stephan of Theirs-Muret expressed it, only those can be called true "poor men of Christ" whose sole possession is God.[31]

While admitting the above similarities, it must nevertheless be emphasized that the view of poverty which the first friars incarnated and which such franciscan sources as the *Sacrum Commercium* expounded far exceeds that of previous and contemporary movements. St. Francis and his followers reminded their contemporaries that an authentic life of poverty consists primarily in emptying oneself of all material and spiritual goods and surrendering one's heart to the Lord. Themes which were only sporadically whispered by earlier groups, such as poverty's intimate relation to the following of Christ, its dynamic function within the history of salvation and its eschatological role in the life of Christians,[32] were loudly proclaimed by the franciscan movement.

By so doing, the Friars Minor re-awakened in the minds of believers the authentic understanidng of Christ's invitation to the young man (Mt 19:21). They also rekindled in the hearts of the faithful the desire to follow Christ's *transitus* to the Father by stripping oneself of all possessions and surrendering oneself totally to him.

b. The External, Ascetical Dimension of Poverty

The franciscan sources examined above consider poverty to be a basic category of the Christian life. For these sources, poverty is the road a person must tred if he is to become transparent to the Lord, to neighbor and to self. Several other sources, however, narrowed this many-faceted concept of poverty to such an extent that only its outer, physical shell remains evident.

In the papal documents, for example, poverty appears most frequently as that aspect of the friars' life which must be clarified, modified and dispensed from. The friars' life of poverty means primarily that they "fled" temporal goods and freed themselves from the "vanities" of the world, that they inhabit such houses as are built for them and wear the religious habit. It must nevertheless be pointed out that the popes continually reminded the friars that they adopted and live this poverty "for the sake of Christ."[33]

The papal documents make it clear, futhermore, that even in the earliest decades of the Franciscan Order both the *practice* as well as the *interpretation* of poverty underwent a very significant evolution. For Francis an actual renunciation of material goods was an important aspect of poverty. According to the papal declaration *Quo elongati,* however, poverty was interpreted to mean not so much the renunciation of things, but rather the renunciation of the *right* of possessing things. Thus the friars surrendered "dominion" or ownership, but were allowed the "use" of things.[34]

The later franciscan sources continued this trend of *externalizing* poverty. The Four Masters, for example, maintained that the friars are bound to observe "perfect" evangelical poverty. By this they meant that they were to have no fixed possessions, could exercise only the use of things and were to go begging for alms.[35] Though Hugh of Digne readily admitted that evangelical poverty is primarily an attitude of heart, he did not discuss this aspect at length. Rather, he stressed the external signs which authentic poverty demands, such as the wearing of poor clothing, going about barefoot and not accepting money. What he demanded of the friars was an "extreme" poverty, which included the total renunciation of possessions and the begging of alms.[36]

Jordan of Giano connected the concept of "evangelical poverty" with such externals as the renunciation of possessions and the wearing of simple clothing. In the view of Salimbene, becoming a Friar Minor meant selling one's goods, giving to the poor and henceforth not possessing anything. Begging, he maintained, is improtant for these men of poverty, for it reminds them of their constant dependence on the providence of God.

Thomas of Eccleston also emphasized the practice of external poverty. The description he gave of Brother Salomon reminds the reader of the behavior of hermits or early monks. "So strictly did he [Salomon] adhere to the established form of poverty," wrote the chronicler, "that he at times carried in his caperon some meal or salt or small figs for some sick brother and under his arm some wood to build a fire; he very diligently took care that he would not accept or retain anything above the limits of the *most pressing necessity.*"[37]

With great satisfaction, too, did Thomas quote the opinion of Brother Albert that three things made the Order great, namely, "the bare feet, the poor quality of our clothing, and the rejection of money."[38] Each of these items, it is obvious, is an expression of strict, external poverty. At times, such zeal for external poverty even led the English friars to excess. At Shrewbury, for example, Brother William the minister, in his enthusiasm to observe perfectly the intention of St. Francis, had the stone walls of a dormitory removed and replaced with walls of mud. This was done, reports the chronicler, tongue in cheek, "with remarkable devotion and gentleness and *at great expense.*"[39]

* * * *

What has occurred in these sources is a drastic narrowing of vision. In a word, these authors compressed the many-faceted concept of poverty as envisioned by Francis, the *Sacrum Commercium* and other sources, into a one-dimensional reality. Franciscan poverty thereby lost its biblico-spiritual underpinnings and became limited to its ethical, ascetical level. In this context poverty came to mean, primarily, not possessing material goods, inhabiting poor houses, being content with simple clothing and food and even begging for alms. This, it should be noted, is a necessary but first level only of the kind of "emptying" one's heart before God which St. Francis demanded of his followers.

But one must not be overly critical. These works, after all, were products of the 1240's and the 1260's. Hence it is not surprising that they no longer burn with the enthusiasm of the first generation sources. But even more to the point is the very nature of the works. These authors did not set out to repeat the fundamental ideal of St. Francis in all its splendor; this ideal they took for granted. Rather, their purpose was much more specific and down-to-earth. The papal documents and the exposition of the Four Masters were mainly casuistic works whose primary purpose was to solve concrete doubts and problems concerning the day-to-day practice of poverty. The chroniclers, on the other hand, sought to record how the friars lived in various times and places. Given this context, it is quite understandable why such a narrowing of vision in regard to poverty occured in these sources.

This trend of externalizing poverty is significant, for it serves as a historical bridge which links these earlier sources with various controversies which erupted within the Order toward the end of the thirteenth century.[40] The Spirituals, for example, though they lived in different regions—in the Marches of Ancona, in the Provence and in Tuscany—were all united by a common bond, namely, their vibrant desire to live according to the strict observance of the rule. By this they primarily meant living in strict, external poverty, yes, even in destitution.

To achieve this ideal they rejected convents, privileges and prestige, and stressed absolute poverty, humility and simplicity. Attempting to be faithful to these strict and "original" ideals at any price, however, the Spirituals by and large came to adopt a rebellious attitude against their more accommodating religious superiors. By so doing they inadvertently lost sight of a very important aspect of Francis' poverty of spirit, namely faithful obedience to all religious authority, both in the Order and in the Church.

c. Minority

It must be noted, however, that the reality corresponding

to the inner, spiritual dimension of poverty was not completely lost in these later sources. What seems to have occured is
rather a differentiation and specification in the use of terms.
The earlier sources most often used the term "poverty" to
include *both* its outer and inner dimensions. In the *latter*
sense, poverty was often interchangeable and almost synonymous with the term "humility." The later sources, however
tend to limit the term "poverty" to its external dimension.
Its inner dimension, that is, as an attitude of heart, was now
no longer labelled "poverty" but rather "humility" or "minority."

This use of terms is particularly evident in the writings of
Hugh of Digne. For him the term "minority" implies an
attitude of humility and lowliness. One is truly *minor* when
he consciously embraces the lowly and flees the lofty. Such
a person avoids arrogance, whether in word, deed, or apparel.
He never puts himself on display and never considers himself
greater than another. Rather, he has deep respect for all persons, irrespective of their status. Because he has renounced
his own will, he is obedient to everyone. Such an attitude,
says Hugh, is the most characteristic virtue of the Friars
Minor.[41] This, of course, is the very same attitude which St.
Francis demanded of his followers; the saint, however, most
frequently labelled this attitude "poverty," namely poverty in
spirit.

The chronicles seem to continue Hugh's use of terms. Jordan of Giano, for example, maintained that *simplicity* and
humility are the primary characteristics of the Friars Minor.
For Thomas of Eccleston simplicity and humility were an inner attitude of heart and spirit which included a deep openness to the working of the Spirit in the lives of the friars.
To remain authentic, however, this inner attitude must be
fortified by a life of outward poverty. Finally, Salimbene
stressed that the Friars Minor are *parvuli*, that is, lowly and

humble men who depend upon the Lord for their subsistence.[42] In all three cases this inner attitude can be identified with what Hugh of Digne termed "minority," but what was referred to most frequently as "poverty in spirit" in the earlier sources.

2. The Narrowing of Evangelical Perfection to Poverty

In the majority of sources examined, the terms "evangelical perfection," "living according to the form of the holy Gospel," and "following in the footsteps of Christ," are rich in meaning. Their content often embraces such elements as preaching, poverty, the salutation of peace, freedom of eating and drinking, simplicity in words, and inner devotion. Though poverty is always considered a central value, particularly in its relation to the following of Christ, it shares its position of honor with these other evangelical elements.

A few of the sources, however, concentrate on poverty and have a tendency to omit the other evangelical elements. By so doing they greatly narrow the original concept of evangelical perfection to the point of almost identifying it with "poverty." Pope Honorius, for example, labels the life of the Friars Minor as *paupertas*.[43] By so doing he implies that the term "poverty" adequately expresses all their ideals and their striving for evangelical perfection. Jordan of Giano seems to use the terms "evangelical poverty" and "evangical perfection" indiscriminately. Both terms express the renunciation of possessions and simplicity of dress.

St. Clare is a particularly good example of this trend. She was so absorbed in meditating on the poor, suffering Christ that she came very close to identifying the "following of Christ" with living in poverty. In her Rule she declared her desire and readiness to observe "the Holy Gospel of our Lord Jesus Christ."[44] But this concept, too, she closely bound up with fidelity to poverty. At first glance it seems surprising that Clare placed so much emphasis on the external, ascetical aspect of poverty, more even that did St. Francis, whose "plant" she called herself.

It must be borne in mind, however, that Clare's writings are of rather late origin. Celano's biography of St. Clare was written in the 1250's while her own writings stem from the 1230's and 1240's. In other words these writings were authored twenty, thirty and even forty years after her conversion to the "Gospel life." One might therefore pose the question whether Clare placed the same emphasis on external poverty already during the formative, largely unrecorded years of her conversion. Is it not possible that during this early phase of her religious life she viewed her Gospel ideal in more general, biblical terms? Perhaps she began to associate this concept so closely with poverty only in later years, say after the death of St. Francis. This is certainly a possibility.

But more to the point is the fact that many elements of the Gospel life, such as preaching penance, going about barefoot, using the greeting of peace and observing the freedom of eating and drinking, were directly connected with the friars activity as itinerant preachers. Since Clare and her sisters did not have the opportunity to practice this *external* apostolate, it is readily understandable why she ommited mentioning these evangelical elements in her writings.

The sisters' apostolate, centered about contemplation, communal charity, silent suffering and the practice of poverty, was carried on within their convent walls. They embraced this apostolate of the inner life and of poverty so zealously because it was their best and perhaps only way of "following Christ" within their given historical context.

In this connection it should be remembered that the sisters exercised their *inner* apostolate not only for their own sanctification, but also for the spiritual welfare of others. They were conscious of their relationship to—and influence on—people living in the world. The sisters prayed, denied themselves and practiced poverty with a view to benefitting the whole Church, after the manner of the Apostole Paul (Col 1:24; 1 Cor 3:9). This thought rings out clearly in Clare's letter to Agnes of Prague: "I hold thee to be a co-worker of his glorious Body,"[45] that is, the Church.

The above words come close to revealing the beauty of Clare's personality and, indirectly at least, her relationship to poverty. These themes are pinpointed even more vividly in the following passage of her Testament: "Love one another with the *charity of Christ*, and let the *love* which you have in your hearts be shown outwardly by your deeds that, inspired by this example, the Sisters may always grow in the *love of God* and in *mutual charity*."[46] What these words make clear is that the energy which powered Clare's life came not from poverty but rather from love, that is, love of God and neighbor!

It is love, she writes, which makes it possible for God to dwell in the soul. To become God-like and to enjoy the sweetness of the Lord already in this life, one must love and love deeply. "Love Him in complete surrender Who has given Himself up entirely for thy love," Clare advises Agnes. Then, "thou wilt contain Him by Whom thou and all things are contained, thou wilt possess that which by contrast to the passing possessions of this world thou shalt possess more lastingly."[47] Indeed, the Christian life consists in loving God and Christ with one's whole heart!

If love was so important for Clare, one might ask, what role did *poverty* play in her life and teaching and why did she stress poverty so much? A very satisfactory answer to this problem is given by Celano when he writes: "In frequent words she [Clare] impressed on the Sisters that only then would the community be *pleasing to God* when it was rich in poverty. . . ."[48] In this context God and only he is the *goal* of religious life. Poverty, however, is an important, even a necessary *means* of reaching this goal and of becoming "pleasing to God."

For Clare, then, poverty, even strict external poverty, never became an end in itself, but always remained a means of becoming like Christ and of reaching out for the Kingdom. "So strict was the pact she [Clare] thus entered with holy poverty," writes Thomas of Celano, "and so great the love she had for it, that she would have naught else but the *Lord Jesus* nor wished her daughters to possess aught besides. The most precious pearl of heavenly desire, which she had bought by selling all, could not be possessed, she would say, together with a gnawing worry over temporal things."[49]

In short, in Clare's view poverty has a *functional* value: it helps its followers to fight successfully against the evil one. It leads them along the "narrow path" and through the "narrow gate" into the Kingdom of heaven. Indeed, it helps Clare herself and each one of her daughters to become a "sister, bride and mother" of Jesus Christ himself. When Clare speaks of "the way of poverty," she understands by this expression nothing less than a surrender of one's heart to God in total love, a process which includes exchanging the transient values of this life for the permanent riches of eternity![50]

* * * *

Though the above trend of narrowing the concept of evangelical perfection to poverty is only marginally noticeable in the sources examined, it is definitely not without its historical significance. At the least, the trend serves as a reminder that even such fundamental concepts as "evangelical perfection," "Gospel life," "following Christ," and "poverty" were more of less fluid in the early decades of the Order. They were open to growth and to diminution, to expansion and to narrowing.

Moreover, by isolating poverty as a particularly important aspect of the friars' life, the above trend signals the beginning stage of what was later to become the most burning and controversial issue within the Order, namely the relationship of poverty to the life of the friars and to evangelical perfection itself. During the closing decades of the thirteenth century, poverty was discussed and disputed from almost every angle: the renunciation of "dominion," the nature of "use," "poor use," "moderate use," the vow of poverty, the legitimacy of mendicancy, the limits of dispensation from the rule, and the absolute poverty of Christ and his disciples.[51] As a result of these often heated controversies, poverty—at least in theory—came to be identified more and more with the life of the friars and with evangelical perfection itself. Slowly, the friars came to assume that "the life of voluntary poverty was the way of perfection."[52]

But it is important to note that while this theoretical identification between poverty and evangelical perfection was taking place, the majority of the friars began to live a modified, at times even a lax form of poverty, significantly different from that practiced by Francis. These modifications, to a great extent, resulted from the papal abrogation of the Testament of St. Francis and from the papal distinction between the *use* and the *possession* of goods. This trend was continued by Bonaventure, who considered the renunciation of dominion, by the individual as well as the community, as the highest form of poverty.[53]

As a result of the above evolution in the *practice* of poverty, the typical friar, already during the generalate of Bonaventure, was "no longer the wandering evangelist who worked in the fields, tended the sick, slept in barns and churches, a simple, devout, homely soul content to take the lowest place and be *idiota et subditus omnibus*, but a member of a religious house, well educated and well trained, a preacher and director of souls, a man whom the community could respect and whose services would be valued."[54]

Notes

1. 1 Celano, 22 (Omn, 247). See also M. D. Lambert, *Franciscan Poverty: The Doctrine of the Absolute Poverty of Christ and the Apostles in the Franciscan Order 1201-1323* (London, 1961), pp. 52 ff.

2. Leg 3 Comp, 29 (Omn, 917). See also 1 Celano, 24; 2 Celano, 15.

3. See, for example, Leg 3 Comp, 22 (Omn, 912).

4. 2 Celano, 56 (Omn, 411).

5. Cajetan Esser, *Repair My House,* ed. Luc Mely, trans. Michael D. Meilach (Chicago: Franciscan Herald Press, 1963), p. 73.

6. For further treatment of franciscan poverty, see Esser, *Repair My House,* pp. 73-92; Lambert, pp. 31-125; Lazaro de Aspurz, "'Appropriato' et 'expropriato' in doctrina s. Francisci," in *Laurentianum,* 11 (1970), 3-35.

7. For this characterization of poverty I am indebted to Esser, *Repair My House,* p. 73.

8. See *Rule of 1223,* ch. 2 4, 6.

9. See *Admonition 14* (Omn, 83); *Rule of 1221,* ch. 17 (Omn, 44); *Rule of 1221,* ch. 7 (Omn, 37); *Admonition 11* (Omn, 82).

10. *Rule of 1221,* ch. 17 (Omn, 45). See also *Admonition 7, 8, 17, 28* (Omn, 80 ff.).

11. Esser, *Repair My House,* p. 81.

12. Rightly does W. Busenbender call St. Francis "the saint of the Incarnation." See WissWeish, 15 (1952), 1-15.

13. See *Letter to the Faithful* (Omn, 93); *Adomonition 1* (Omn, 78); *Letter to a Chapter* (Omn, 105).

14. Esser, *Repair My House,* pp. 91-92.

15. Sophronius Clasen has addressed himself to this question in a number of important studies. See for example his article, "Vom Franziskus der Legende zum Franziskus der Geschichte," in

WissWeish, 29 (1966), 15-29.

16. See for example 2 Celano, 65, 66, 67, 68.

17. *Rule of St. Clare,* ch. VIII, 2 (Brady, p. 75).

18. *Vita s. Francisci,* 9 (AnalFranc X, 340).

19. See *Vita s. Francisci,* 16, 19.

20. See *Vita s. Francisci,* 22, 26. That the franciscan observance of poverty was accompanied by a deep joy is attested to by the writtings of St. Francis, the *Legend of the Three Companions,* Jordan of Giano and Thomas of Eccleston.

21. *Sacrum Commercium,* 3 (Omn, 1550).

22. Ibid., 4.

23. For the meaning of poverty in this early franciscan classic, see Lapsanski, pp. 72-76.

24. 3 Celano, 1 (AnalFranc X, 271).

25. K. Balthasar, *Geschichte des Armutsstreites im Franziskanerorden bis zum Konzil von Vienne* (Munster, 1911), p. 57.

26. *De perfectione evangelica,* q. 2, a.l, concl. (Opera Omina, V, 129 A).

27. Ibid.

28. Ibid.

29. See L. Hardick, "Armut (kirchengeschichtlich)," in RGG I, 624-27.

30. *Liber sententiarum seu rationum s. Stephani* (PL 204, 1104).

31. See E. d'Ascoli, "La vita spirituale anteriore a San Francesco d'Assisi," in CollFranc, 2 (1932), 154.

32. Esser, *Repair My House,* pp. 89-92.

33. For a treatment of poverty in these papal documents, see Lapsanski, pp. 209-14.

34. See Lambert, p. 127.

35. Four Masters, ch. 6 (Oliger, p. 158).

36. See Lapsanski, pp. 172–75.

37. Thomas of Eccleston, *Chronicle,* ch. 3 (Hermann, p. 103).

38. Ibid., ch. 14 (Hermann, p. 168).

39. Ibid., ch. 4 (Hermann, p. 115).

40. See Moorman, pp. 188–92.

41. For a treatment of minority in the writings of Hugh of Digne, see Lapsanski, pp. 170–72.

42. *Cronica* (Scalia, pp. 30, 421).

43. *Cum secumdum consilium* (BullFr, 6).

44. *Rule of St. Clare,* ch. I, 2 (Brady, p. 66).

45. *Third Letter to Agnes,* 3 (Brady, p. 93).

46. *Testament of St. Clare,* 18 (Brady, p. 86).

47. *Third Letter to Agnes,* 3 (Brady, p. 94).

48. *Legend of St. Clare,* 13 (Brady, p. 28).

49. Ibid.

50. *First Letter to Agnes,* 5 (Brady, p. 90).

51. See Lambert, p. 245.

52. Moorman, p. 318.

53. See Lambert, pp. 126 ff.

54. Moorman, p. 154.

6.

ST. FRANCIS
AS THE FULFILLMENT OF
EVANGELICAL PERFECTION

In a previous section of this study we examined the almost arrogant self-concept which the early franciscan community had of itself and its mission. In that section, too, a number of reasons were offered to explain this surprising feature of the primitive community. Another reason why the Friars Minor had such a positive and confident image of themselves lies very likely in the person of St. Francis himself. The saint, after all, was greatly loved by all segments of society and, almost immediately upon his death, he came to be venerated by the official Church.

This joyful scene which Thomas of Celano paints so vividly must have occurred numerous times, when Francis traveled through the Italian villages and towns, preaching penance and love of God: "So great was the faith of the men and women, so great their devotion toward the holy man of God, that he pronounced himself happy who could but touch his garment. When he entered any city, the clergy rejoiced, the bells were rung, the men were filled with happiness, the women rejoiced together, the children clapped their hands; and often, taking branches from the trees, they went to meet him singing" (1 Celano, 62; Omn, 281). What Celano does here is to interweave the theme of Christ's triumphal procession into Jerusalem with the description of an Italian "fiesta" in order to recount the people's love for Francis. For his part, Francis loved the people. This love, as Celano reports, continued even after the saint's death: "From the east and from the west, from the south and from the north those come who have been helped through his [Francis'] intercession. . . . Everywhere he is helping everyone; everywhere he is at the behest of everyone . . . " (1 Celano, 119; Omn, 334).

Because such a great saint was their own founder and brother, the friars must have soon come to the realization that theirs was an Order of unique importance and that their function consisted in carrying out the mission which God himself entrusted to Francis. It is therefore fitting to conclude this study with a summary of how the early sources viewed the person and mission of this great saint and founder of the movement which bears his name. Here again we will be dealing not so much with biographical data, but rather with theological reflection.

1. St. Francis and Salvation History

The encyclical letter of Brother Elias, in which he announced to the Friars Minor the death of their father and brother, contains a dramatic theological interpretation of the person and work of St. Francis of Assisi. Because Francis, blind and on the verge of death, blessed his sons on his deathbed, he resembled the patriarch Jacob, Elias declares. Because of the wounds Francis bore in his body, he became for those who saw him an image of the Man of Sorrows. Moses brought to the people of Israel the Ten Commandments and the Covenant; Francis gave to his followers "the law of life" and "the covenant of peace," namely his Rule and Testament. He is therefore a new Moses. Like King Solomon, Francis, too, became renowned throughout the lands. Finally, like John the Baptist before him, so too did Francis come from the "true light." He brought light to those who "sat in darkness" and prepared for the Lord "a new people."[1]

A number of the sources continue and even deepen this typology. According to 1 Celano, for example, St. Francis was like John the Baptist and the apostles because he bore "witness" to the truth by his preaching and way of life. He was the "new evangelist" and the "new man" through whom a "new spirit" was poured out on believers.

With these words filled with biblical imagery Celano re-

flects on the mission which Francis fulfilled for the Lord:
"For in this last time this *new evangelist,* like one of the
rivers that flowed out of *paradise,* diffused the waters of the
Gospel over the whole world by his tender watering, and
preached by his deeds the way of the Son of God and doctrine of truth. Accordingly *in him and through him* there
arose throughout the world an unlooked for *happiness* and
a holy newness, and a shoot of the ancient religion suddenly
brought a great *renewal* to those who had grown calloused
and to the very old. A *new spirit* was born in the hearts
of the elect, and a saving unction was poured out in their
midst, when the *servant and holy man of Christ,* like one
of the lights of the heavens, shone brilliantly with a *new
rite* and with *new signs"* (1 Celano, 89; Omn, 304). Truly,
to the people who saw him and came into contact with him,
the Poverello seemed like "a new man, one from another
world."[2] Francis became a "new man" and at the time an
instrument for bringing about "newness" and "renewal" to
the world, because of his openness to the Lord and his
fidelity to the life of the Gospels.

Continuing the same train of thought, Julian of Speyer
compared Francis to Moses, who led his people out of
Egypt, to Elijah, who left his gift of prophecy to his follower
Elisha, and to Jacob, who blessed his sons on his deathbed.[3] Finally, the Bull of Canonization called St. Francis
the "laborer" whom God sent into the vineyard of his
Church at this "eleventh hour." Because of his lowliness
and simplicity, Francis resembled Noah's ark as well as
Samson who used the simple jawbone of an ass to conquer
his enemies. Because of his deep faith, moreover, St. Francis was like the patriarch Abraham, while in his dedication to prayer he resembled Jacob.[4]

Still other sources portray Francis as a special instrument
of God and invest him with an almost salvational role. To

him, declare the liturgical texts, God gave a throne of glory as he did to King David. Him did God establish as his "witness" to the nations. Like Israel of old, Francis, too, served as a lawgiver and leader of nations (Is 55:4). Francis, designated the standard-bearer of the eternal King and the legate of Christ, convoked a mighty army to wage war against the heresies which plagued the Church of his day. Protected by the shield of faith, helmeted with hope, armed with the sword of the Word of God and girded with the belt of chastity, this mighty champion scattered the heretical followers of the fierce dragon of the Apocalypse. Having nobly fulfilled his mission, St. Francis, now the glorious victor, was received into eternal glory by Christ the King.[5]

Jacobus de Voragine, the dominican preacher, also had some significant things to say about Francis. Like the Angel of the Apocalypse (18:1), so too did Francis bring heavenly light to the world. By his teachings the saint illumined those who were in darkness. By his example he inflamed the tepid and by his miracles he converted the obstinate. Just as St. John the Baptist preceded the first coming of Christ, a coming in mercy, so in the present age did God send Francis as the forerunner of Christ's second coming, a coming in justice.[6]

It is interesting to note that St. Bonaventure, who called St. Francis the Herald, the Knight, the Servant of Christ, the Herald of Christ's Gospel, and the Proclaimer of Christ's Cross, also attributed to Francis the mission of being Christ's forerunner. According to Bonaventure's theology of history, the sixth and final age of the world extends from the first coming of Christ till the end of the world, which will be signaled by Christ's second coming. Bonaventure can therefore view Francis as Christ's forerunner, not in the sense that Bonaventure expected a proximate return of Christ, which he did not, but in the sense that by his life and teaching Francis renewed mankind and helped lead it to Christ.[7]

2. The Conformity of St. Francis to Christ

The early sources declare with enthusiasm that St. Francis resembled the great personages of the Old and New Testaments. With even greater enthusiasm do they proclaim the Poverello's similarity to Christ himself. Indeed, that Francis closely resembled Jesus Christ is a theme which underlies the entire *Vita II* of Thomas of Celano. "I think Blessed Francis was a most holy mirror of the sanctity of the Lord," Celano writes, "and an image of his perfection. All his words, I say, as well as his deeds are redolent of the divine . . . " (2 Celano, 26; Omn, 385).

In the above quote Celano views the life of Francis as something which was already finished. Writing some twenty years after the death of St. Francis, Celano reflects upon the kind of person Francis became and declares solemnly that he was indeed an "image" and "mirror" of the Lord's perfection. But, one is led to ask, when did this process of becoming like Christ begin for Francis? What were the highpoints of this life-long spiritual journey?

The answers to these fascinating questions are provided by Thomas of Celano himself, but also by other early sources, for example by the *Legend of the Three Companions* and by Jacobus de Voragine.[8] These sources emphasize that the process of becoming like Christ began in the life of Francis when he encountered the Crucified in the Church of San Damiano. In this personal encounter the Suffering Christ, so to speak, imprinted his own image on the very soul of Francis. This experience filled him with the "greatest joy and inner light because in spirit he knew that it was indeed Jesus Christ who had spoken to him." Francis was deeply touched by the Lord; his life was for ever after changed and changed radically. "From that hour," Francis' companions testify, "his heart was stricken and wounded with melting love and compassion for the passion of Christ; and for the rest of his life he carried in it the wounds of the Lord Jesus" (Leg 3 Comp, 14; Omn, 904).

From then on Francis became pre-occupied with Jesus. And the rest of his life can be explained as a continuous process of becoming transformed into his Lord. "This was proved later," the companions continue, "when the stigmata of those same wounds were miraculously impressed upon his own holy body for all to see" (Leg 3 Comp, 14; Omn, 904). Thus did he become the "crucified" servant of the "crucified" Lord.[9] The stigmata which appeared on Francis' body at the end of his life were merely the external manifestation of an already long-present inner reality, namely Francis' deep love for Jesus Christ.

This same theme is emphasized also in Celano's *Treatise on the Miracles.* Because the entire life of Francis revolved about the "mysteries of the Cross," Celano states, he came to bear the likeness of the "body of the Crucified."[10] The liturgical texts, too, call Francis the "friend of the Crucified." The saint's stigmata were brought on by the keen love he felt throughout his life for the suffering Christ. As a result of this dynamic love operating within him, Francis was transformed into the very image of his beloved.[11] In death, Salimbene emphasizes, Francis truly seemed "like a crucified man taken down from the cross."[12]

A few of the sources went even further in expressing the intimate relationship between Francis and Christ. In fact they come very close to identifying the one with the other. Brother Elias, for example, maintained that Francis was a "true light" who came into the world (Jn 1:9). Like Christ, he preached the Kingdom of God and brought peace to his people (Eph 2:17). He bore the very wounds of Christ so that he himself appeared "crucified"[13] (Gal 6:17).

In similar fashion, though less directly, 1 Celano associated Francis with Christ by stating that his presence was like a "light" (Jn 1:4ff.; 3:19) sent from heaven. "It seemed at that time, Celano reports, "whether because of the presence of St. Francis or through his reputation, that a *new light* had been sent from heaven upon this earth, shattering the wide-spread darkness that had so filled almost the whole region that hardly anyone knew where to go" (1 Celano, 36; Omn, 259).

Even more dramatic is the viewpoint expressed in 2 Celano (Omn, 536). Here the author reports how Francis cele-brated his own passing to the Father by repeating and mak-ing present the Last Supper of the Lord Jesus. Francis "blessed and broke" bread which was brought to him; he then "gave a small piece of it to each to eat." He had the Passion of the Lord read to him from the Gospel of John. In this way Francis, identifying himself very consciously with the Lord Jesus, wished to leave his followers a "memorial" of himself; he wished thereby to show "the deep love he had for his brothers." Only when all these "mysteries of Christ" were "fulfilled" in Francis did he depart from this life.

Even that is not the end of the story. Celano goes on to report a vision granted to a brother in prayer. The brother saw the "glorious father" Francis clad in the "purple dal-matic" of a deacon and accompanied by a vast multitude of men. A few men separated themselves from the multitude and asked the brother, "Is this not Christ, Brother?" He answered that it was. But then the multitude asked him, "Is this not St. Francis?" He again answered that it was. Cel-ano concludes this report with these words: "Indeed, it seemed to the brother and to that great multitude that Christ and Blessed Francis were *one and the same person.*"

This is indeed a strong, even shocking, statement. One

would therefore expect Celano to soften its impact, since he is here dealing with a vision and since he is very conscious that many persons would be very sceptical about this kind of near identification of Francis with Christ. But Celano does no such thing. In his personal reflection he rather re-enforces the impact of the vision. The close identification of Francis with Christ, Celano declares, "does not seem to understanding people to be in any way a rash judgment, for he who cleaves to God is made one spirit with him, and God will work all things in all" (2 Celano, 219; Omn, 538). Basing himself on the doctrine of St. Paul, Celano in effect tells his readers that there is nothing shocking about the vision he reports. Rather, this is what salvation is all about, becoming "one spirit" with the Lord (1 Cor 6:17). This is precisely what happened to Francis!

The process of spiritual growth which St. Paul described as taking place within his own life is noticeable also in the life of St. Francis. The following words which St. Paul spoke of himself can with almost equal right be said of Francis: "I reckon everything as complete loss for the sake of what is so much more valuable, the knowledge of Christ Jesus my Lord. For his sake I have thrown everything away; I consider it all as mere garbage, so that I might gain Christ, and be completely united with him. . . . All I want is to know Christ and to experience the power of his resurrection; to share in his sufferings and become like him in his death, in the hope that I myself will be raised from death to life" (Phil 3:8-11). Francis, the early sources declare, did become like Jesus in life, in death, and even beyond death!

* * * *

The above typology, of course, is nothing radically new. Stephan of Thiers-Muret[14] and Gerald of Salles were compared to John the Baptist because of their strict asceticism. Because of his effective preaching, too, the same Gerald was called another Apostle Paul.[15] Moreover, Stephan's biographer at times referred to him as "soldier of Christ" and "man of God." Then, too, a number of persons, for example, Robert of Arbrissel and Norbert of Gennep, were called "apostolic men." These leaders in turn applied such titles of honor as "imitators of the apostles," "imitators of Christ," and "poor men of Christ" to their own followers.[16] In addition, various groups of heretics considered themselves to be "vicars of the apostles."[17] All these references, however, seem quite superficial when compared with the rich and extensive biblical imagery which the franciscan sources applied to St. Francis.

In this connection St. Dominic offers a much closer point of contact with St. Francis. In the Bull of Canonization, for example, Pope Gregory IX compared Dominic to two figures of the Old Testament, namely to the obedient Samuel (1 Sm 3) and to the loving Daniel (Dn 10:11).[18] Another source called Dominic a "new vessel" (2 Kgs 2:20) which Christ used in order to save many people from their sins. Moreover, in his preaching Dominic resembled Jacob, while in his contemplation he was another Israel. Because of his life of grace and ability to pass judgment, he resembled Elijah.[19] In his prayer life he was another Moses.[20] Indeed, the abbot Joachim seems to have clearly predicted the coming of Dominic and his Order. Just as the patriarch Jacob entered Egypt with his twelve sons, so would Dominic enter and illumine the world with twelve leaders of his Order.[21]

As regards biblical personages, then, the above sources seem to predicate of St. Dominic much the same thing as the franciscan sources predicated of Francis. But there is no indication that the dominican sources emphasized resemblances between Dominic and Christ, a theme so dear to the franciscan authors. In this regard St. Francis seems to be unique.

* * * *

What the early franciscan sources intended by emphasizing so many parallels between Francis and biblical personages was to show that the saint, and consequently also the Order he founded, can only be adequately explained within the framework of Salvation History. Francis was viewed as the embodiment of the "perfection" of both the Old and the New Testaments. He did for the people of his generation what Jacob, Abraham, Moses, David and John the Baptist did for theirs! In his life and mission he resembled Jesus Christ himself. In this perspective Francis and his brothers were viewed as a very special instrument in the hand of God which he is using to bring about the salvation of mankind. And the "evangelical life," which Francis and the brothers so well incarnated, is the dynamic power which pushes Salvation History forward!

Notes

1. *Encyclical Letter* (van Corstanje, pp. 125-128). For a closer analysis of this text see Lapsanski, pp. 61-63.

2. 1 Celano, 82 (Omn, 297). See also Esser, *Repair My House,* pp. 15-45.

3. See *Officium s. Francisci,* 24, V (AnalFranc, X, 386); *Vita s. Francisci,* 29, 68.

4. *Mira circa nos* (BullFr, 42-4).

5. See *Fregit victor,* 1, (AnalFranc X, 403); *Caput draconis,* 5-6 (AnalFranc X, 401).

6. *Sermo 2* (TestMin, 107 ff.).

7. See Sophronius Clasen, "Die Sendung des hl. Franziskus. Ihre heilsgeschichtliche Deutung durch Bonaventura" in WissWeish, 14 (1951), 224.

8. See 2 Celano, 10-11; Leg 3 Comp, 13-14; *Sermo 1* (TestMin, 105).

9. *Vita s. Gregorii IX* (AnalFranc X, 100, n. 16).

10. 3 Celano, 2 (AnalFranc X, 272).

11. *Legenda Umbra,* 2 (AnalFranc X, 544); *Fregit victor,* 13-14 (AnalFranc X, 404).

12. *Cronica* (Scalia, p. 282).

13. *Encyclical Letter* (van Corstanje, pp. 125-28). See Lapsanski, pp. 63-43.

14. *Vita s. Stephani* (PL 204, 1023 f.).

15. ActaSS, Oct. X, 255, 258.

16. See PL 162, 1053, 1091; MGSS, XII, 678, 681, f.

17. See Grundmann, p. 95, n. 46.

18. *Fons sapientiae* (BullRom III, 184).

19. See B. Altaner, *Der hl. Dominikus. Untersuchungen und Texte* (Breslau, 1922), pp. 240 ff.

20. See M.-H. Vicaire, *Saint Dominique de Caleruega d'apres les documents du XIIIe siecle* (Paris, 1955), p. 270.

21. See Altaner, pp. 240 ff.

Conclusions

The purpose of this study was to extract from the early franciscan sources the fundamental values about which the life of the primitive community revolved. An allied purpose was to indicate the evolution many of these values underwent during the decades here in question. Having done this in previous chapters, I now wish to summarize the entire study by presenting a number of conclusions concerning the life and values of the early franciscan community.

1. With great unanimity the sources declare that the religious life led by St. Francis and his companions was grounded on and sprang from a personal experience of God. It was the Lord who brought about the conversion of Francis and revealed to him the kind of life he was henceforth to live. It was the Lord who gave Francis brothers and who formed them into a "new people," by his tangible presence in their lives. For their part the brothers responded to the Lord by being open, by surrendering their hearts to him and by being thankful for his loving kindness.

2. St. Francis wanted to live the whole Gospel of Jesus Christ and not merely one or another part. For Francis such an observance of the Gospel centered about the great commandment of love, love of God and neighbor. Francis and the earliest sources, especially Thomas of Celano and Julian of Speyer, also connected the Gospel life with the

123

literal observance of Christ's words to his apostles as he sent them out to preach. Hugh of Digne and the *Legend of the Three Companions,* among others, broadened the concept of "Gospel Life" by adding other evangelical elements to it. Other sources, for example, St. Clare, the Four Masters and the chronicles, narrowed and de-emphasized the concept "Gospel Life" because of their different historical situation and the specific purpose of their writings.

3. There is considerable evidence for maintaining that St. Francis was acquainted with the ideals and teachings of the Cathari and even with the Waldenses. There is also a possibility that he came into contact with other apostolic groups, such as the Humiliati, the Poor Catholics and the Community of Bernard Primus. One is therefore led to conclude that though Francis' fundamental inspiration for living the Gospel came from the Lord, it is nonetheless possible that at least some aspects of his life-style and teaching may have been influenced, whether directly or indirectly, positively or negatively, by these other contemporary apostolic groups.

4. No doubt, the image of the humble, poor, crucified Christ so uniformly presented by the franciscan sources must have been in part influenced by earlier religious revivals, for example the itinerant preachers of France, and by the Crusades. This image, however, was personalized and refined by Francis' own vivid experience of the Crucified Christ in his life.

5. Because of this specialized image, Francis and the early community came to identify the following of Christ primarily with an internal emptying of self and a complete surrender to the Lord, combined with an external surrender of all material goods and values. Other sources came to stress especially the external practice of poverty. St. Clare and 1 Celano also associated the following of Christ with a

mental re-living of his earthly life.

6. It is significant that such terms as "apostolic life" and "life according to the form of the early Church" play only a very peripheral role in the early franciscan sources, whereas they are very prominent in the pre-franciscan movements. Perhaps by avoiding these terms Francis and his companions wished to disassociate themselves from the slogans of these apostolic groups, some of which clearly rejected the authority of the Church. More to the point, however, is the fact that the early franciscan sources preferred to use such terms as "to follow in the footsteps of Christ." This is so because Francis and his companions wished to follow and to imitate not the apostles or other saintly persons, but Christ himself. It was the person of Jesus Christ who was the friars' "way" to the Father.

7. The friars' Gospel way of life deeply influenced the view they formed of their community and their mission. Using biblical categories, a number of the sources described the order as a "new nation," a "new Israel," a "new People of God." The friars viewed themselves as having been invested with an important spiritual mission, namely to be faithful to the Gospel life which the Lord revealed to Francis. By being *minores,* the friars were able to show others how to follow Christ. It was the Lord himself, they felt, who sent them to transform the "old world" corrupted by sin and thus to lead many people to salvation.

8. The early sources emphasize that poverty was always a very important aspect of the friars' life of evangelical perfection. But the authors' understanding or view of poverty underwent a significant evolution during the decades here in question. The earliest sources, for example St. Francis and the *Sacrum Commercium,* viewed poverty as a fundamental attitude of the entire person. External poverty was viewed by them as the visible expression of a much deeper

and broader reality, namely inner poverty or poverty in spirit. Later sources by and large came to concentrate on the external, ascetical aspects of poverty. The term "evangelical perfection" came to be narrowed in later decades to mean the "perfection of evangelical poverty."

9. The early sources also contain significant theological reflections on the person and work of St. Francis. For example, they compared him to the patriarch Jacob, to the Man of Sorrows, to Moses, to Abraham and to John the Baptist. They viewed Francis as the Legate of Christ and the Champion of the Word. In fact, because of his deep love for the Lord, declare the sources, Francis came to resemble Christ himself very closely. This typology and theological reflection reveal that the early franciscan authors were very conscious of God's continued and loving intervention in man's history. They viewed Francis and his brothers as special instruments which God is using to accomplish his plan of bringing mankind to himself. All this is happening today, in the contemporary age, the sources declare.

* * * *

Francis and his brothers, I believe, can best be viewed as the thirteenth century incarnation of the paradox proclaimed long before by St. Paul. The paradox is that God's wisdom is foolishness to man, that God's strength operates best through man's weakness, that the Cross brings life.

It's almost as if St. Paul had Francis and his first followers in mind when he wrote these unsettling words: "Few of you were wise, or powerful, or of high social standing, from the human point of view. God purposely chose what the world considers nonsense in order to put wise men to shame, and what the world considers weak in order to put powerful men to shame. He chose what the world looks down on, and despises, and thinks is nothing, in order to destroy what the world thinks is important. This means that no one can boast in God's presence. But God has brought you into union with Christ Jesus, and God has made Christ to be our wisdom; by him we are put right with God, we become God's holy people, and are set free. So then, as the Scripture says, 'Whoever wants to boast must boast of what the Lord has done!'" (1 Cor 1:26–31).

St. Francis and his followers were not wise or powerful by human standards. Rather, they were weak and little. But they had an overwhelming sense of God's greatness. And this great God they viewed and loved as a Gift-giver who showers them with life, with joy and freedom and brings them to himself through his Son Jesus. The friars felt themselves to be God's "holy people"; they boasted not in themselves but in the Lord and what he has done for them. They were true "lesser brothers"!